38 John Aldridge

The goalscorer extraordinaire enjoys the banter as he debates whether his LFC Scouse XI would beat Peter Reid's EFC Scouse XI

53 The result

Who won the fantasy derby, or did it end all square?

CONTENTS

Sport Media
A Trinity Mirror Business

WRITTEN BY: Simon Hughes
PRODUCED BY: Jamie Dunmore & Roy Gilfoyle

EXECUTIVE EDITOR: Ken Rogers
EDITOR: Steve Hanrahan
ART EDITOR: Rick Cooke
PRODUCTION EDITOR: Paul Dove

WRITERS: Chris McLoughlin, David Randles, Gavin Kirk, John Hynes
DESIGN TEAM: Lee Ashun, Barry Parker, Colin Sumpter, Glen Hind, Alison Gilliland, James Kenyon

PHOTOGRAPHY: Trinity Mirror, Action Images
PRINTERS: Pensord
SALES & MARKETING MANAGER: Elizabeth Morgan
0151 285 8412
Write to: Sport Media, PO BOX 48, Liverpool, L69 3EB

Tommy SMITH

Terry McDERMOTT

Jamie CARRAGHER

Liverpool Football Club's
SCOUSERS

'My view of Scousers is simple. If you confront them, they will confront you back. No danger about that. But if you hold out a hand of friendship, you will get friendship back ten times over' - **Tommy Smith**

THIS magazine is unique. Never before has a publication sought to give a special salute in one volume to the Scouse (or Merseyside) giants who have proudly worn the red of Liverpool Football Club.

That thought in itself is enough to make the hairs on the back of your neck stand up, stirring memories of Smithy, Cally, Chris Lawler, Gerry "Crunch" Byrne and Tommo, supported by 21st century Scouse giants like Stevie and Carra.

But this is not just a trip through the glorious history books. It is fantasy football at its most potent.

In the pages that follow, one of those true Scousers – John Aldridge – will study the complete squad list of Liverpool FC's Merseyside hall of fame and select his starting eleven and substitutes for a derby of derbies against Peter Reid's Everton FC Scouse XI played in front of the soaring stands of the new Wembley Stadium.

Aldo will take you into the dressing room; conduct an inspirational team talk; fantasise about the scene in the players' tunnel and then play in the greatest Merseyside clash of all time.

It's a game and an occasion that will blow your mind, especially in Liverpool's Capital of Culture year.

For now, we pose two simple questions; Why is football so important to Scousers and what makes Scouse footballers so special?

If you think of Scousers on the pitch it will usually inspire images of decorated legends winning the biggest prizes the game has to offer.

Whether it's Phil Thompson or Steven Gerrard parading European Cups, it doesn't really matter because when people picture Scousers in their head, a newly acquired trophy is usually gleaming close by, backed up by an incomparable history.

Ask Steven Gerrard or Jamie Carragher what it is like performing at Anfield and they will tell you that whether it's the brilliant highs or desperate lows, they revel in the emotion that goes with pulling on a red shirt much more than players from outside the area.

It is true that all players feel the same personal joy or disappointment, but for Stevie and Carra victory means adulation from family, friends and anyone they meet in the street.

Defeat, and the same people are on your case.

Also in these pages we ask Phil Thompson what it means to be a Scouser representing his hometown team, we speak to Jan Molby about being an honorary Scouser, David Fairclough tells us about being a Scouser abroad and we get the celebrity diehard Red view from The Farm's Peter Hooton.

There is no escape from football in Liverpool because everyone is so obsessed and consumed by it. Most of all, it defines our identity.

What is a Scouser?

Scouse: Brit informal noun
1. Also called: *Scouser* - a person from Liverpool.
2. The Liverpool dialect (adj).
3. of Liverpool, its people, or their dialect (from lobscouse a sailor's stew)
from Collins English Dictionary

SEFTON

ST HELENS

LIVERPOOL

KNOWSLEY

WIRRAL

Liverpool - anyone born and brought up in this area is definitely a Scouser

Merseyside - anyone born and brought up in this area is more debatable, but in this exercise is eligible for the Liverpool FC Scouse XI

BEFORE we get you on the edge of your seat, we need to discuss the boundaries for this derby of derbies.

It is difficult deciding whether certain players can be defined as Scouse because there are several variations that could identify the exact borders of Scouseland.

If a Scouser is someone who resides in Liverpool, consulting the Merseyside FA guidelines will tell you to discount clubs or players from Wirral.

Yet if you research phone numbers, parentage or education, it will extend and redefine the margins.

Many people within certain borders may not believe they are Scousers, but others in the same area may have parents or siblings that carry the Scouse gene, and therefore consider themselves to be a patron of Liverpool.

There are, of course, varying levels of Scouseness. Some would say that the further away from the city you were born and brought up, the less Scouse you are.

It is the subject of much debate, but for the purpose of this magazine we have identified Scouseland as an area stretching from the northern hinterlands of southern Southport, down towards the eastern outskirts of Kirkby and Huyton, and across to southern Wirral in the west.

In short, we are including any player who was born inside what is currently known as Merseyside as a Scouser.

Tommo

Phil Thompson
Interview

The European Cup winning captain on living the dream of every Scouse Reds fan

Interview by **SIMON HUGHES**

THE LIVERPOOL squad are heading home after a rare away defeat midway through the 1970/71 season.

Bullets of rain batter the windows amid squally conditions as the team bus trawls up the motorway.

Inside the atmosphere is surprisingly snug, jovial even, with a number of players laughing and joking on the back seats.

Then a vexed Tommy Smith emerges from his seat and the spirit dampens.

All of a sudden, the atmosphere in the bus makes the weather outside seem calm.

Striding purposefully from his position close to the management, he approaches the rear of the coach.

"The laughter was quite evident. It surprised me because we had just lost," recalls passive onlooker Phil Thompson.

"So Smithy, in his usual calm and understanding manner, walked up and said: 'Who the effing hell do you think you

> **'We'd play a game of football every spare minute of the day. Even when it was 20-a-side we'd all want to win'**

are, laughing and joking?' He says: 'This is all about winning, one thing and one thing only. This should be hurting you. This has cost me my bonus this week and it's not good enough, so don't be effing laughing because there's nothing to effing laugh about.'"

Thompson anticipated anxiously as Smith sludged back to his seat with an air of calmness out of line with his previous ire.

"I was only a young boy at the time and to witness that was serious stuff. On the pitch he demanded commitment from everyone. If anyone did anything wrong, he would bollock you and when he did anything wrong, everyone would just say 'Unlucky Tommy.'"

Although he admits that he was unnerved by Smith's rage on the bus that day, such competitiveness had already been instilled into Thompson years earlier.

Growing up in Kirkby, Thompson would play on a nearby field until nightfall, sharing a plastic fly-away ball between eight families.

Every player wanted to win and losing, even amongst his teenage friends, wasn't an option.

"There were no second sports at home; football was the only sport. We'd play a game every single spare minute of the day that we had. Even in games when it was 20-a-side, everyone would want to win."

When there were fewer kids around to play, Thompson would engage in a spot of, well 'spot' – the kind of game that he says is sadly missing from the streets today.

He explains: "There would be one area

Tommo
Phil Thompson
Interview

Thompson

Tommo playing for Liverpool in the FA Cup in 1980

of a wall, which would be really small and you would have to hit it. Then the person you were playing against would have to hit the spot again wherever the ball bounced. If you missed, you would be on the letter S and then P and so-forth until the word SPOT was completed.

"It was good for improving technique because in one touch you would have to get it under control and pass it. You don't see enough kids playing this kind of game any more, and that is one of the reasons why we are behind in basic skills. Kids have Playstations and X-Boxes to play on instead and it's taking kids' minds away."

There was no such time for anything but football as Thompson grew up. He was obsessed with playing, as were the rest of his mates.

"There was talent coming out of the walls, especially in places like Kirkby, Huyton and Toxteth. It was a pleasure and an honour to play for your town team. Back then, each town had their own team, it wasn't like it is now with borough teams like Knowsley, which stretches from schools in Halewood to Huyton, taking in a number of towns.

"It was really healthy because it gave young lads a sense of local pride and honour. Added to that, there used to be leagues like the Kirkby New Town League, then the Kirkby & District League, which would alone have five divisions."

Thompson's sense of local pride has always been obvious to Kopites and this was ingrained from an early age.

"I played Sunday league, school football, five-a side, district, town football; I was playing for all these teams. There was nobody from an academy telling me I couldn't play for who I wanted to.

"This is a problem. They're becoming stars at the age of 9, 10 and 11 because they play at an academy.

"They are strutting round their schools and other kids look at them as too much of a hero, so they're losing all sense of reality and, even more importantly, relevant social skills.

"When I grew up, I didn't care where I played, whether it was in the street, on the

'There was talent coming out of the walls, especially in places like Kirkby, Huyton and Toxteth. It was a pleasure and an honour to play for your town team'

field or in the yard at school. It didn't matter to me."

The fact that Thompson was still playing for Kirkby Boys as well as his Sunday league side at the age of 15, either shows you how times have changed or that the future Reds captain was a late developer.

Like so many Scousers who have made it to the top level of football with one of Merseyside's premier clubs, he had a brief flirtation with the other before signing for the Reds.

Training at Bellefield on Tuesday and Thursday nights, Thompson was with Everton for around six months, but as soon as Liverpool came calling, in his own words, he "jumped ship".

There were no contracts to stop him doing what he wanted to do back then and before long he was at Melwood nearly every day.

"Melwood at the time was full of young local lads. There were amateurs and trialists and teams who would come down and play every night. One of the first games I played in for Liverpool was against a Kirkby Sunday team called Medbourne and we won 5-2 and I scored two. I played centre-midfield. I must have made an impression, but it was hard to because there must have been more than

Phil Thompson, pictured in his playing days, goes back to his roots and the fields in Kirkby where he spent so much time playing football

Tommo learns his lesson – and takes cup to the pub with him

IT'S early evening on May 28, 1981. A purple Ford Capri speeds down Liverpool side streets towards Kirkby.

Inside Phil Thompson is entertaining a special passenger. The European Cup rattles slightly on the back seat.

Twenty-four hours earlier, Tommo was lifting 'ol' big ears' in Paris after Alan Kennedy's 81st minute strike had defeated Real Madrid.

Every Kopite has been told a different story about how Phil Thompson took the European Cup back to Kirkby. This is what really happened:

"It's become legend now, especially since 2005 when Stevie ended up winning it. I was captain when we won the League Cup final replay at Villa Park (against West Ham). We brought the cup back on the coach and had a good time. The next morning, I had a phone call off Peter Robinson and he said: "Phil, we have a problem. What happened to the League Cup?", so I said: "What do you mean, what happened to the League Cup?". He then explained that it had been left on the bus over night, so he had to go to the bus depot in the morning and pick it up. So I asked him what he wanted me to do about it. Peter then said: "You're the captain, you should have taken care of it and taken it home." Then he put the phone down.

"So when we won the European Cup, I didn't need to be told twice. So after we had done the tour round the city on the Thursday, I saw all my mates from the Falcon, and told them to go back to the pub and wait without telling them why. They thought we were just going for a party.

"When I got off the bus I got the cup and hid it and put in the back seat of my car and took it quickly back to Kirkby. Everyone seemed to be waiting in the pub; family, friends and everyone I knew. The place was awash with Liverpool fans, there was red everywhere and by that point all the lads had returned from Paris. It was an incredible time, just incredible. The celebrations went on and on.

"I remember telling all the mums and dads to bring their kids back the next morning at 11 o'clock when the pub opened so they could have their picture taken with the cup. Then I got a call at 9am from Peter Robinson: "Phil, do you know where the European Cup is?" So I am there with a stonking hangover and I remember looking at the mirror on the sideboard in my room. I am sure there were about four European Cups behind me because my eyes were that blurred. I told him that I had it in my bedroom and he wasn't happy because the world's press were waiting to take pictures. Straight away I thought 's***' because I remembered promising all the people at the Falcon. I kept my word though and took it for half and hour and got it back to Anfield for 12 o'clock. Peter never said a thing."

100 kids, even at night time. Melwood was packed with great footballers with talent everywhere."

Thompson was informed in the summer of 1970 that he would have six weeks to earn a contract. At the same time he completed the same duties as other players who had already signed apprentice forms. It was a nervous time for the future Liverpool captain.

"Even if I had left after those two years, the experience I had was truly unbelievable. For a young kid, a Kopite, to be rubbing shoulders with Ron Yeats, Ian St John and Roger Hunt, who was my hero, it was special. What made it even better was that you got to meet Bill Shankly. Not that I talked to him, he would talk to me. No young lad would make conversation with the great man; he would do all the talking. It would always be about your welfare, 'How are you son?' 'Are you eating well, are you sleeping well?'"

Shankly wasn't the only person keen to make him feel at home in his new surroundings with the first team squad.

"The whole squad were great with me. Everyone took care of me, especially the Scouse lads. I always remember getting in

a scrape at Man City with Franny Lee and Rodney Marsh because I had a little kick at somebody. Clive Thomas was the referee and before I knew it, everyone was piling in. Of course, Smithy came to my rescue and really took care of me. He was threatening and pointing the finger at all the City players and he got me out of the s***. Tommy got booked and warned by Clive, but he kept on going on at him and got sent off.

"There was a pecking order at Liverpool. The new ones who came into the team had to do all of the fetching and carrying. If we were ever on a European trip, the young lads would always have to go to the bar and collect the drinks for the older players. That was part of the upbringing, but it was the right way to do it and I thought it was a pleasure having to do it."

According to Thompson, this kind of system doesn't exist now.

"It's definitely changed. The game is always changing. It changed from the 60s to the 70s and 80s when I played and it's changing again now. I think with the foreign influence in every I club, I think all the players care and they really do care about whether they win or lose, but I don't think they care enough. That's the slight difference. I know they all really want to do

>

BEST OF SCOUSE

We ask Tommo to rate the Scousers in the Liverpool dressing room

Best Scouse player
"The most influential Scouse player was Tommy Smith. Tommy was the epitome of what I call a Liverpool player. He never, ever understood the word defeat. He wanted the best out of himself and his colleagues."

Funniest Scouser
"Terry McDermott. Terry was a legend. He was naturally a funny guy. All the players were very serious on the pitch, but off it we loved a laugh."

Scouse party animal
"Me and Terry Mac would be out; Jimmy Case and Sammy Lee; Tommy and Cally would all have a good time out on the town. That was the camaraderie amongst the players. We played at the greatest time with Liverpool Football Club and we always partied with the fans."

Streetwise Scouser
"I would like to put myself in that bracket because I was always one step ahead of them, especially when I was reserve team manager. I had been there and I knew what all the young lads would try and do. All the young apprentices would try and pinch boots and training gear, but I would catch them out because I tried the same things."

Plastic Scouser
"There are so many really. I mean this in a good way because he just embraced the city, but Jan Molby definitely."

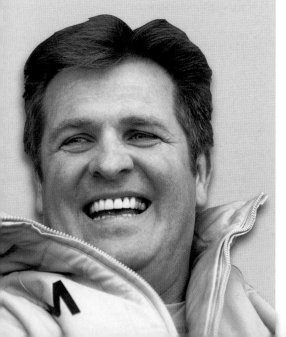

well, but they will never have the same feelings the local lads did or have.

"When you're a local lad, you're out and about more often. You're in touch with the fans all the time. There's no escaping being a local lad, whereas the foreign lads usually mingle in their own select groups and that's it, so they don't get the real feelings of elation when you win and the real depression when you lose."

Thompson admits he was lucky to have featured in Liverpool's greatest ever era through the 70s, so he didn't endure too many days of despondency.

Quite the contrary. By the time he was 22 years old, Tommo had already lifted the league title (1973), UEFA Cup (1973), and the FA Cup (1974). He could scarcely comprehend that he was at the forefront of all this glory.

"I couldn't believe what was happening. I was playing in arguably the club's best ever side, a side that was on the verge of greatness, and I was playing a big part in it. I kept asking myself how I managed to get where I was but there was no time to really sit back and smell the roses because the games and trophies came and went. 1978/79 was the most complete side at the club. We had an astonishing group of players who came together at the right ages – 25, 26, 27, 28 year olds all coming together at their peak."

If Thompson felt lucky to have experienced the good times with playing a captaining role in arguably the Reds' best ever team in 1979, he certainly appreciated it years later when he finally left the club and signed for Sheffield United.

"At first, the Sheffield people were alright. Everything was going well. We saved them from relegation in the first few months, but after that it went downhill.

"People would call me a Scouse this and that all the time. I certainly felt victimised because I got absolutely slaughtered. They'd all be there on the touchlines trying to ridicule me: "You're a has-been, you're finished, you're this, you're sh***, you're a big nose, Scouser this, Scouser that," they

> ### 'I couldn't believe what was happening. I was playing in arguably the club's best ever side, a side that was on the verge of greatness, and I was playing a big part in it'

would shout. Every time you would even just go to pick up a ball which had gone out for a throw-in, you would get it, especially off quite a few home fans at Bramall Lane."

Since retiring from the game in 1985, Tommo has returned to the club in two spells under Kenny Dalglish and Gerard Houllier.

He admits that one day he would fancy a return to the club again in some capacity. But for the time being, he is happy just meeting up with some of his former team-mates.

It was at one of these recent gatherings that Thompson realised how privileged he was to have shared so much success with fellow local lads. It certainly won't be the same in the future for Scousers of today.

"We had a former player Christmas Party and I was thinking what it's going to be like in 30 years' time. The foreigners coming in are all going to move on. There's only going to be Stevie and Carra sitting there. Who's going to be left? It's a horrible feeling. When I thought about the pride that we have in our former players' association, the pride that we have for our football club, it was quite disturbing thinking about the future."

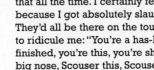

THE ULTIMATE MERSEYSIDE DERBY

EVERTON

VERSUS

LIVERPOOL

DEAN · ROONEY
LABONE · HARVEY

GERRARD · FOWLER
SMITH · CALLAGHAN

COMPETING FOR THE TITLE OF **THE GREATEST MERSEY SIDE** OF ALL TIME

SOLD OUT

WEMBLEY STADIUM, LONDON

PREPARE FOR A SCOUSE INVASION AS THE CAPITAL OF FOOTBALL COMES TO THE CAPITAL OF ENGLAND

The ideal man to handpick the Liverpool FC Scouse XI

JOHN Aldridge may have been donning a blue jumper when we met up with him at a watering hole in Liverpool's docklands, but there's no doubting which colour his loyalties lie with come Merseyside derby day.

A red through and through, John Aldridge is the ideal person to select and manage an all-time Liverpool FC Scouse XI.

That's because he's seen it all.

Made to wait for a chance to play for the club he supported as a boy, Aldo took the long route from his Garston home across town to Anfield.

It took years of grafting in lower league football before he was handed the opportunity to grace Anfield wearing Liverpool red.

Almost a decade of wanting went by, playing at Newport Town and Oxford United, before he was finally given recognition for his goalscoring achievements when Kenny Dalglish signed him in 1987.

He may have only stayed at Anfield for two years, but a goalscoring record of more than one in every two games cemented his place in club folklore.

After experiencing an equally successful spell in front of goal in Spanish football with Real Sociedad, Aldo returned to England with Tranmere Rovers where he reached second in their all-time leading scorers list, despite playing in the twilight of his career.

Eventually, he took over as Rovers' manager, taking them to the unchartered territory of the League Cup final.

Today, he still resides in the city and works as a well respected radio co-commentator covering Liverpool matches.

But we've given him another taste of football management by handing him the task of picking his best XI from the list of Scousers who have represented the Reds over the years.

The list of players he has to choose from appears on the next page and it's up to you to decide whether his fantasy team is the best Scouse XI he could have come up with.

"I wouldn't describe it as an altogether happy memory for me because I was leaving the club I loved – and the club I had always dreamt of playing for – but to get the chance to score at the Kop end in my last game was special. It was a very poignant moment for me. Everyone knew I didn't want to leave. I'd have stayed there for the rest of my career if I could…"
- John Aldridge on leaving Liverpool

Jamie CARRAGHER

Steven GERRARD

Robbie FOWLER

ROLL OF HONOUR

From Alan A'Court to Stephen Wright, here is the full list of Merseysiders to have represented the Reds that John Aldridge had to choose from. Who would make it into your Liverpool FC Scouse XI?

Alan A'COURT	Don CAMPBELL	Matthew FITZSIMMONS
Gary ABLETT	John CARLIN	Robbie FOWLER
John ALDRIDGE	Willie CARLIN	Tom GARDNER
Jack BALMER	Len CARNEY	Howard GAYLE
John BAMBER	Jamie CARRAGHER	Steven GERRARD
Alan BANKS	Jimmy CASE	Tom GREEN
Tom BENNETT	Phil CHARNOCK	Alf HANSON
Arthur BERRY	Francis CHECKLAND	Chris HARRINGTON
Louis BIMPSON	Albert CHILDS	John HEYDON
Robert BLANTHORNE	John DAVIES	Dave HICKSON
Phil BOERSMA	Joe DICKSON	Alan HIGNETT
Thomas BRADSHAW	Cyril DONE	Alan HIGNETT
Tom BROMILOW	John DURNIN	Ralph HOLDEN
Derek BROWNBILL	Roy EVANS	Jason HUGHES
Gerry BYRNE	David FAIRCLOUGH	Laurie HUGHES
Ian CALLAGHAN	Phil FERNS	Colin IRWIN
Bobby CAMPBELL	Fred FINNEY	Norman JAMES

David JOHNSON	Johnny MORRISSEY	Jamie SMITH
Barry JONES	Bobby MURDOCH	Mark SMYTH
Harold JONES	John NICHOLSON	John SPEAKMAN
Charlie JOWITT	Jon OTSEMOBOR	Sammy SPEAKMAN
George KAYE	Stan PALK	Eddie SPICER
Brian KETTLE	Jack PARKINSON	David THOMPSON
Kevin KEWLEY	Jimmy PAYNE	Phil THOMPSON
Frank LANE	Lee PELTIER	Max THOMPSON
Chris LAWLER	Steve PEPLOW	Fred TOMLEY
Sammy LEE	Keith PETERS	Harold WADSWORTH
Henry LESTER	Darren POTTER	Walter WADSWORTH
Harry LEWIS	David RAVEN	William WATKINSON
Doug LIVERMORE	John ROBERTS	Alex WATSON
Thomas LOWRY	Syd ROBERTS	Henry WELFARE
Thomas LUCAS	Tom ROGERS	John WELSH
Jason MCATEER	Arthur ROWLEY	Johnny WHEELER
Terry MCDERMOTT	Colin RUSSELL	John WHITEHEAD
John MCKENNA	Dave RYLANDS	Bryan WILLIAMS
John MCLAUGHLIN	Alan SCOTT	Don WOAN
Steve MCMAHON	Mark SEAGRAVES	Arthur WORGAN
Steve MCMANAMAN	John SEALEY	Stephen WRIGHT
Tony MCNAMARA	Les SHANNON	
Joe MALONEY	Bill SHEPHERD	
Mike MARSH	Danny SHONE	
Jimmy MELIA	Tommy SMITH	
Bill MOLYNEUX	John SMITH	
Ronnie MORAN	Sydney SMITH	

For more details on the players on this Scousers roll of honour turn to page 82

Frank LANE

1 Frank Lane
Goalkeeper

D.O.B 20/07/1948
Liverpool Career Apps 2 (1972)

NOT to be confused with Chicago-born jazz/gospel singer Frankie Laine, Frank Lane hailed from Wallasey and enjoyed a short, but memorable, career with Liverpool in the early 1970s.

Unlike Laine, who was billed as Mr Rhythm, our Frank was unfortunately not blessed with anywhere near as much coordination.

On his debut at Derby, in September 1972, Frank distinguished himself for all the wrong reasons by collecting an innocuous looking cross before stepping backwards over his goal line.

Liverpool lost the match as well, 2-1, so it was a decisive mistake.

ALDRIDGE: There haven't been many Scouse goalkeepers who have played many games over the years. Initially, I was going to pick Tony Warner, but then I realised that he never actually made an appearance for Liverpool. He was on the bench for something like 200 consecutive games, which is crazy really. So, I had to choose Frankie Lane. I remember his mistake all those years ago, and I suppose that is the only thing that makes him stand out from the others.

'There haven't been many Scouse goalkeepers, but Frank's mistake makes him stand out in my mind'

Why has Merseyside produced so few goalkeepers?
Aldo and Reid have their say

Page 45

Which goalkeepers missed out? Bill Molyneux, Charlie Jowitt

Phil THOMPSON

4 Phil Thompson
Centre-back

D.O.B 21/01/1954
Liverpool Career Apps 477 (1971-83)
Liverpool Career Goals 13

PEOPLE say the Dutch created 'Total Football', but most Liverpool fans would argue that it was us that laid the foundations.

Phil Thompson arrived at Melwood as a ball-playing midfielder, so when Bill Shankly converted him to a centre-back, his continental credentials shone through.

Shanks banned Ray Clemence from taking long goal kicks and ordered him to release the ball short to the full-backs or indeed Thompson or his partner Emlyn Hughes.

This encouraged expansive passages of controlled play and made the Reds' style of football easy on the eye to observers.

Thompson's elegant style didn't mean he couldn't mix it up though. Despite being labelled 'matchstick legs' by Shankly, he was also fierce and determined in the challenge.

A born leader, he captained his boyhood favourites to domestic and European glory between 1979 and 1982.

ALDRIDGE: With Tommo and Smithy at the back, I think I have the perfect blend. I'd want Smithy to attack anything in the air and Tommo to sweep and play. Smithy can play too because he was great on the ball, but that would be Tommo's main job. He's a proper Liverpool lad, a Red through and through, and he was a good talker too. He'd get the lads going in the changing rooms and tunnel and I am sure he'd try and wind some of the opposition up too.

> 'Tommo's a proper Liverpool lad, a Red through and through, and he was a good talker too. He'd get the lads going in the tunnel'

Which centre-backs missed out?

Gary Ablett, Tom Bromilow, Jamie Carragher, Laurie Hughes, John Haydon, Walter Wordsworth

Smithy parading the 1973 league championship trophy

Tommy SMITH

10 Tommy Smith
Centre-back

D.O.B 05/04/1945
Liverpool Career Apps 638 (1963-78)
Liverpool Career Goals 48

THE QUINTESSENTIAL Scouse footballer, Tommy Smith was born barely yards away from Anfield.

With the blur of an angry chainsaw, the tough defender was as sharp with his tongue as he was in a 50-50 challenge.

As tough in the tackle, he was also technically sound and had leadership skills to rival a war commander.

It would be fair to say that they don't come any more Scouse than Tommy.

He may not have lifted the European Cup as a captain, but he scored a towering header against Borussia Moenchengladbach as the Reds lifted their first European title in 1977.

If fans are wondering why Tommy has been issued with the number 10 shirt in this team, then it's down to Bill Shankly.

Shanks issued Tommy with the shirt halfway through the 1964-65 season in an attempt to confuse opponents. It seemed to work.

Tommy kept the shirt for a year-and-a-half as Liverpool swept to title glory in 1966.

ALDRIDGE: When I think of Scousers to have played for either Liverpool or Everton, no player is more Scouse than Tommy Smith.

No player has ever given as much to Liverpool Football Club as Tommy. He cared so much and wouldn't accept second best.

He was as hard as nails and nobody ever crossed him twice, because if you crossed him once, his reaction alone would scare the s*** out of anyone. Having said that, he may have been hard, but he was fair too and would rarely get involved in trouble unless it was merited.

Sometimes I think people overlook just what a good player he was because he was so hard. Technically he was spot-on and always offered a goal threat from corners, free-kicks and from the penalty spot. He simply has to be the captain of the side.

'No player has ever given as much to Liverpool Football Club as Tommy. He cared so much and wouldn't accept second best'

2 Chris Lawler
Right-back

D.O.B 20/10/1943
Liverpool Career Apps 549 (1960-75)
Liverpool Career Goals 61

Chris LAWLER

IF CHRIS Lawler played today, the only full-back that would come close to him in terms of records is Cafu.

The Brazilian legend and World Cup winning captain would be good enough to just about polish his boots.

Lawler scored more than 60 goals in over 500 appearances for the Reds – quite a feat, given that he didn't take free-kicks or penalties. Cafu has scored 15.

Even Roberto Carlos' 57 club career goals from left-back can't match Lawler's impressive haul.

Whether or not another full-back anywhere in the world can boast 'The Ghost's' impressive strike rate is doubtful.

Unlike Cafu or Carlos, who explode forward in dynamic style at every opportunity, Lawler was an understated and economical defender, who went about his business with stealth, thus earning another nickname, 'Silent Knight'.

Lawler also managed to miss only three out of 336 league matches between 1965 and 1974.

ALDRIDGE: On the right hand side Chris was a match winner for us because nobody ever picked him up. His goals-per-game ratio was phenomenal. There was no-one better in his day than Chris at ghosting in at the back post. Phil Neal's goalscoring record was great but, with all due respect, a lot of his goals were penalties.

> 'His goals-per-game ratio was phenomenal. There was no-one better at ghosting in at the back post'

Which full-backs missed out?   Ronnie Moran, Robert Done, Jason McAteer

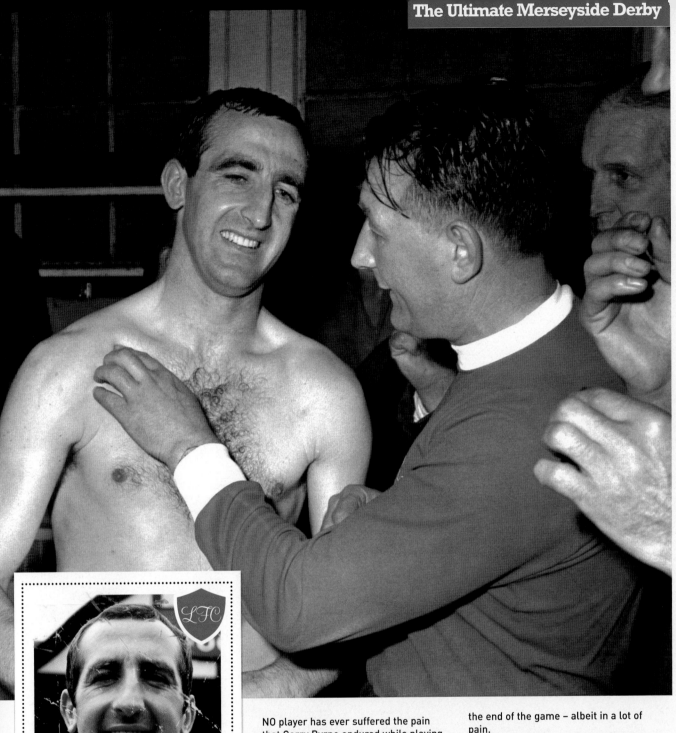

Gerry BYRNE

3 Gerry Byrne
Left-back

D.O.B 29/08/1938
Liverpool Career Apps 333 (1957-68)
Liverpool Career Goals 4

NO player has ever suffered the pain that Gerry Byrne endured while playing for Liverpool. Literally.

It's not because Byrne, who spent his whole career at Anfield, experienced heartbreaking cup final defeats, or spent long spells on the sidelines during trophy-laden seasons.

No, his career followed exactly the opposite path in fact, and he was a mainstay at left-back while Bill Shankly revolutionised the club.

The real reason why he suffered was because he played more than 117 minutes of the 1965 FA Cup final with a broken collarbone after a horror challenge from Leeds United captain Bobby Collins.

He even managed to set up Roger Hunt's opening goal, and although Leeds managed to equalise, Ian St John's winner meant that Byrne could just about manage to lift the trophy at the end of the game – albeit in a lot of pain.

Byrne's influence on the game was a factor not lost on Shanks, who said: "Gerry's collarbone was split and grinding together, yet he played on in agony. It was a performance of raw courage from the boy."

ALDRIDGE: I remember the time Bobby Collins mullered him in the 1965 cup final. It was on TV the other day. It was honestly the worst challenge I have ever seen in football. It was bad that one (stands up), Gerry's running with the ball, and Collins goes studs first into his shoulder (whacks his chest). Shanks apparently told Gerry not to show the Leeds players that he was injured because there was only a few minutes gone and there were no subs then. So he's played through extra time and he's running like an idiot. He just shrugged it off; you'd never see that now.

'I'd ask Cally to cut inside all the time and get the ball in the box because there probably hasn't been a better crosser of the ball in Liverpool's history'

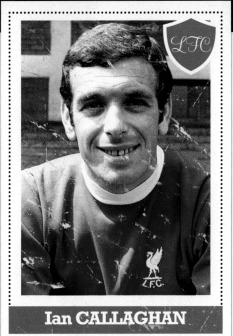

Ian CALLAGHAN

11 Ian Callaghan
Wide midfielder

D.O.B 10/04/1942
Liverpool Career Apps 857 (1960-78)
Liverpool Career Goals 68

LIVERPOOL'S record appearance holder is, quite appropriately, a Scouser.

When Cally first attracted Liverpool scouts at the age of 16, few would have thought that he would serve the Reds over two glorious decades.

One Second Division title, five First Division championships, two FA Cups, two UEFA Cups, one European Cup and a World Cup winners medal are just some of the awards that stand in Cally's bulging trophy cabinet.

He is also the only player whose career spanned the Reds' rise from the mediocrity of the Second Division to European champions.

Upon joining the Reds for a £10 signing-on fee, he was moved from his original position at wing-half, where his 5ft 7in build was considered too small for the rigours of midfield.

He instead became a fast, busy winger who created many scoring opportunities with his accurate crosses.

A wing-back before wing-backs were even invented, Callaghan had such unbelievable energy down the right flank that he was an integral part of the Reds' squad right up until he departed Anfield at the age of 36.

Success, it seemed, followed Callaghan wherever he went as he helped Swansea City to two successive promotions after leaving Liverpool.

His longevity also helped him through his brief international career. Although he only made four appearances for England, he holds the record for the longest wait between caps.

He made his debut against Finland in 1966 before appearing once in the World Cup, but then he fell away from the international scene and it wasn't until 1977, after a vintage season with Liverpool at the age of 35, that he reached his third and fourth caps.

ALDRIDGE: I couldn't pick a Liverpool all-time XI without including Ian Callaghan. Although he's probably going to have to play on the left in this game, he was a brilliant right winger in his day and just seemed to keep going and going. I would ask him to cut inside all the time and get the ball in the box because there probably hasn't been a better crosser of the ball in Liverpool's history.

Which wide midfielders missed out? Jimmy Payne, Kevin Lewis, Alf Hanson, Johnny Wheeler

Steven GERRARD

17 Steven Gerrard
Midfielder

D.O.B 30/05/1980
Liverpool Career Apps 417 (1998-present)
Liverpool Career Goals 90

STEVEN GERRARD is the only Scouser in Aldo's starting XI still playing.

It would be easy to pen the superlatives to describe him, but to put it quite simply, Steven Gerrard is the complete footballer.

Aside from leading Liverpool to Champions League glory for the first time in 21 years, Stevie has every attribute to dominate games at the very highest level.

There is not enough space on this page to mention all the great goals and moments he's had in a red shirt.

Alaves 2001, Everton 2002, Man Utd 2003, Olympiakos 2004, Istanbul 2005, West Ham 2006...the list goes on and it seems he has hauled Liverpool from the depths of despair on at least one occasion every year since he made his debut as an 18-year-old.

He's been there and experienced every emotion while playing for Liverpool, including the highs of the treble season, to the elation of Istanbul. Stevie has been there in the thick of it all.

There is no other player in the world who can be compared to our inspirational skipper at the moment.

Even though England fans would say he hasn't reproduced his club form for his country, it's only Liverpool that we care about and aside from Jamie Carragher no other player has been as consistent for the Reds over the last 10 years.

ALDRIDGE: What a player! Where would we be without him? I have never known a player like him. He's got everything and I love him. Since retiring from playing, Stevie's given me my best moments as a Liverpool fan and the fact that he's the only modern player in my squad shows you how great he is. He could quite easily captain this team; then again so could others like Thompson, but Stevie leads by example on the pitch, so I am going to allow him to focus on his own game. He's had more than enough of dragging other players out of the s*** over the years, so it's about time he had a rest from that!

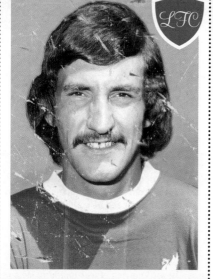

Terry McDERMOTT

20 Terry McDermott
Midfielder

D.O.B 08/12/1951
Liverpool Career Apps 329 (1974-82)
Liverpool Career Goals 81

SCORER of arguably Liverpool's greatest ever goal, Terry Mac was an integral part of the Reds' greatest ever side.

The first player to win the Football Writers' and PFA Player of the Year in the same season (1980), Kirkby-born McDermott was a spectacular midfielder with an eye for goal.

His strike in the 7-0 Anfield victory over Spurs in 1978 was straight out of a Roy of the Rovers comic book.

On a sunny day, he ran fully 70 yards to finish off a sweeping move that started in Liverpool's 18-yard box and finished in the back of Barry Daines' net.

McDermott's success as a player for Liverpool was made all the sweeter because he had to wait for so long to represent the club he supported as a boy.

He made more than 150 appearances for Bury and Newcastle before becoming one of Bob Paisley's first signings in 1974.

But even then, he displayed patience on the fringes of the squad for almost two seasons before really making his mark on the starting XI.

When he did, it coincided with Liverpool's most successful period in their history as the Reds won the European Cup (three times), the First Division (four times), the UEFA Cup and the League Cup (two times).

Terry Mac also lifted the Charity Shield on four occasions as well as the European Super Cup, making his medal haul one of the most impressive in Liverpool FC history.

ALDRIDGE: Terry Mac has to be in the side. What a legend. Underrated too. If he played today, everyone would be going on about him. Just look at Frank Lampard. Although he's not really in the same mould, he won more trophies than Lampard and has a goalscoring record to rival him, so he should have had a lot more recognition of his achievements. All the players loved him too because he was a funny fella.

Which midfielders missed out?

Mike Marsh, Jimmy Melia

Jimmy CASE

7 Jimmy Case
Wide midfielder

D.O.B 18/05/1954
Liverpool Career Apps 269 (1973-81)
Liverpool Career Goals 46

POSSESSOR of arguably the hardest shot from any player in the club's history, Jimmy Case was equally full-blooded in the tackle.

He is also one of the most decorated players in the Anfield annals, racking up four First Division championships, three European Cups, a UEFA Cup and a League Cup in six years at the club.

On the pitch, Case summed up what is great and good about Scouse players.

Tenacious and hard working, the wide-midfield player was also good on the ball and never shied away from possession.

With all the niftiness of a pickpocket, Case would pinch the ball from the opposition and release it with stealth to goalscorers like Keegan, Toshack or Dalglish. Either that or just have a shot himself.

Again, like so many players from his era, Case started his career at Anfield without a hair on his face, but by the time he'd become a full-fledged member of the first team, the little winger had grown an unmistakable full-on Texan across his upper-lip.

Allerton-born, he was a true Scouser in a team of true greats.

ALDRIDGE: Jimmy Case was a hard b****** and I loved him for it. I used to feel sorry for people coming up against him because he must have been a nightmare for full-backs. He'd always get stuck in and he had a ridiculous shot, and that was well documented. But it was the way he allowed players like Dalglish to play that made him really special. His shooting ability was unstoppable and just as good as, if not better than, Stevie G today. Ferocious he was.

'He'd always get stuck in and he had a ridiculous shot, and that was well documented. But it was the way he allowed players like Dalglish to play that made him special'

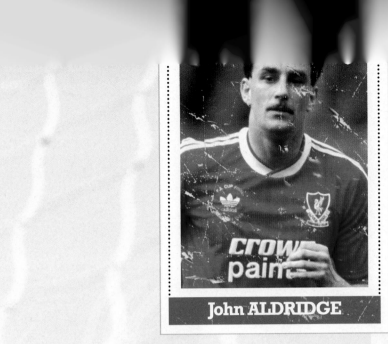

John ALDRIDGE

8 John Aldridge
Striker

D.O.B 18/09/1958
Liverpool Career Apps 104 (1987-89)
Liverpool Career Goals 63

WITH a record that no great post-war goalscorers can match, Aldo only played for Liverpool for two seasons.

But his 63 league and cup goals spearheaded the Reds towards the First Division championship (1988) and FA Cup success (1989).

Signed as a replacement for Juventus-bound Ian Rush, the fervent Kopite had a reputation as a poacher during spells with Oxford United and Newport County.

And he continued to score even after leaving Anfield, netting 40 times in 70 games for Real Sociedad and 174 in 287 games for Tranmere Rovers.

To put it simply, Aldo was the definition of a goal machine, yet he made it look so simple.

Master of link-up play, he would receive the ball with his back to goal, play it into the appropriate channels and move stealthily into the box before finishing with ease.

His achievements as a league manager with Tranmere may have been more modest, but in cup football he enjoyed a memorable run to the League Cup final where he only lost out to Martin O'Neill's Leicester City in 2000.

ALDRIDGE: As a player-manager, it is difficult to focus on your own game while also allowing the rest of the team to get on with theirs. I'd really be looking to work down our right hand side and make sure Chris Lawler is getting down there and exploiting John Bailey's ability to have eight pints the night before the game. With Jimmy Case also on that side, I would look to play on the right of our front two with Robbie using his left-foot.

had he not got so
many injuries he
would have become
our all-time leading
goalscorer'

9 Robbie Fowler
Striker

D.O.B 09/04/1975
Liverpool Career Apps 369 (1993-2001, 2006-07)
Liverpool Career Goals 183

Robbie FOWLER

IT was inevitable that Robbie Fowler would become a goalscoring legend at Anfield.

After all, he had a well-founded reputation as a prodigy in Liverpool's junior leagues well before he hit the headlines.

Fowler scored 16 goals for his Toxteth Sunday league team Thorvald in one game when he was 11.

Lots of kids are tipped for future stardom, but whether a player has scored five hat-tricks (plus one) in a single game is doubtful.

In the mid-90s, there was no striker more prodigiously gifted at finishing even half chances than Fowler.

He scored more than 30 goals in each of his first three full seasons at Anfield, a record only bettered by Newcastle's Alan Shearer.

Fowler also boasts the distinction of scoring the quickest hat-trick in Premiership history.

In 1994, after he found a way through the much-vaunted 'watertight' Arsenal defence, he netted three goals in four minutes and 33 seconds.

If that is not enough, he scored all five goals as the Reds trounced Fulham in only his fourth game for the Reds.

A darling of the Kop, the crowd loved him and labelled him 'God.' No other player in Liverpool's history has received such an accolade.

Like all proper Scousers, Fowler was always up to some kind of mischief, making the front pages for controversial goalscoring celebrations and his notorious feud with Chelsea's left-back Graeme Le Saux.

Despite this, Fowler also won a FIFA Fair Play award after he pleaded with referee Gerald Ashby not to give a penalty against Arsenal after he rode David Seaman's challenge.

Fowler eventually left Liverpool for Leeds in 2001, but was welcomed back five years later after a short spell with Manchester City.

ALDRIDGE: I think me and Robbie would make a great partnership. At his peak, he had that extra bit of pace that gave him the edge over any marker. His record at Liverpool was phenomenal and I have no doubt that had he not got so many injuries, he would have become our all-time leading goalscorer. His style changed over the years and in his second spell at the club he played a little deeper, but in this game, I would want him to be right up the pitch. One thing about Robbie that everyone seems to overlook was his heading ability. He scored a lot of important goals with his head due to his timing, movement and leap, so I would have no hesitation in asking the wingers to get the ball in the box.

Which strikers missed out?

Dave Hickson, Jack Balmer, Cyril Done, Jack Parkinson

Substitutes

5 Sammy Lee
Midfielder
D.O.B 07/02/1959
Liverpool Career Apps 295 (1978-86)
Liverpool Career Goals 19

12 David Fairclough
Striker
D.O.B 05/01/1957
Liverpool Career Apps 154 (1975-83)
Liverpool Career Goals 55

14 Steve McManaman
Midfielder
D.O.B 11/02/1972
Liverpool Career Apps 364 (1990-1999)
Liverpool Career Goals 66

15 Steve McMahon
Midfielder
D.O.B 20/08/1961
Liverpool Career Apps 277 (1985-91)
Liverpool Career Goals 50

16 David Johnson
Striker
D.O.B 23/10/1951
Liverpool Career Apps 213 (1976-82)
Liverpool Career Goals 78

McMahon

McManaman

Jamie CARRAGHER

'It has been my hardest decision leaving Carra out. He's been so good in every position for Liverpool and he'll kill me for this!'

23 Jamie Carragher
Defender

D.O.B 28/01/1978
Liverpool Career Apps 502 (1997-present)
Liverpool Career Goals 4

ALDRIDGE: It has been my hardest decision leaving Carra out. He's been so good in every position for Liverpool, I can't believe I am doing it, but I desperately want my team to score goals. He could play in any of the positions across the back four equally as well, if not better than the players I've selected. Both centre-backs had a partnership so I can't break them up. I was going to play him at right-back, but Chris Lawler's 61 career goals from that position was too good to ignore. Carra will kill me for this! All of the players on the bench have their merits and I know I could call on any one of them at any time.

John Aldridge's
Liverpool FC Scouse XI

Back row (L-R): Frank Lane, Phil Thompson,
Chris Lawler, Tommy Smith, Jimmy Case
Front row (L-R): John Aldridge, Ian Callaghan, Steven
Gerrard, Terry McDermott, Robbie Fowler, Gerry Byrne

SCOUSERS

The Ultimate Merseyside Derby

Aldo's picked his Liverpool FC Scouse XI, but now it's time for the big test. How would that team get on against Peter Reid's all-time Everton FC Scouse XI? It's the derby match fans would flock to see in their millions and we want to know how Aldo and Reidy see the match going. Every aspect of the star-studded match has been discussed, but which team would earn the right to be known as the pride of Merseyside? **SIMON HUGHES** chairs the fascinating debate.

First impressions: Reidy on Liverpool

Peter Reid: Well, I think John has made a massive mistake with his 'attacking' line-up. It's going to be hard to defend against, but with Rooney in that hole, I am not sure who's going to pick him up. Unless...mind you, I have just seen Jimmy Case, so I take that back, because I can see Jimmy trying to get hold of little Rooney in there.

John Aldridge: Come on Reidy, I've got Tommy Smith playing too remember. This game is going to be played in the early 70s, so I'd set Tommy on him. He'd be off after 10 minutes.

PR: There would be no one left on the pitch because everyone would either be getting fouled and injured by Tommy, or getting sent off fighting with him.

JA: Smithy was a great player too though.

PR: Both sides have great players in there. When I look at Gerrard and Terry Mac...I have got to say that I thought Terry Mac was underrated, even though he did win player of the year. And I have got to say...Ian Callaghan.

For my sins I used to watch Liverpool as a kid and when you look at Lawler, Smith, Byrne and Callaghan, they were great players, and I mean top drawer players, so it would be a really difficult game. Also, when you talk about hard men, I have played against Jimmy Case a couple of times and he was hard, but had great ability as well.

JA: He scored goals as well.

PR: He was a goalscorer yeah. You look at the Liverpool side and there's a lot of goals in it. But if Aldo's thinking his team can get at our defence, I think the three we've got in the middle of the park would give us a lot of protection at the back.

JA: Yeah, I'd like to see you chase Terry Mac and Stevie around! (laughs)

PR: Let me tell you, I would find that hard. I remember going away on holiday to Ibiza in 1982 with Terry, going out every night on the piss and getting up in the morning, then chasing him round. Nobody could run with Terry McDermott. He was a runner and a half.

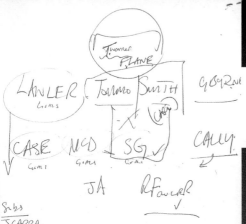

First impressions:
Aldo on Everton

JA: It's a great team to be fair. My big worry
for Reidy is defensively. Watto and Labone,
yeah, Bailey was a good player in his day
and Tommy Wright, but we've got it all
going forward. I think their defence is the
weakness of the side.

PR: What I'd do is defend narrow. I'd defend
narrow and not let them play through us.
Instead, I'd make them go wide and get
crosses in. That Aldridge and Fowler would
never win anything in the air against Labby
and Waggy. I rest my case. In fact, we'd just
boot everything out for throw-ins and
corners, then we'd just boot it long, get it up
the pitch and into the box, then Dixie would
get on the end of it...bang, 1-0.

JA: That would be a battle royale between
Dixie Dean and Royle, and Smithy and
Tommo. I'm just deciding what to do with
Rooney. I think Stevie would have to do the
sitting. I'd tell him to keep his eye on
Rooney, cos we've got Jimmy Case and
Cally providing from wide.

PR: Yeah, but I'm glad you have got Cally on
the left hand side and I'd get Tommy Wright
to show him inside all the time... and then
smack him (laughs) cos that's the only way
you'd stop Cally.

JA: It really is intriguing when you look at it,
with Reidy going with three up front and me
with two.

'That would be a
battle royale between
Dixie Dean and
Royle, and Smithy
and Tommo'

Team Line-ups

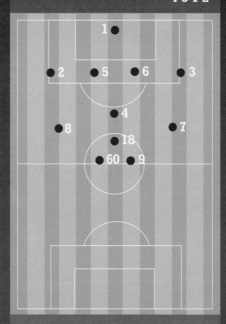

EVERTON
4-3-1-2

LIVERPOOL
4-4-2

EVERTON	LIVERPOOL
1. Andy Rankin	1. Frank Lane
2. Tommy Wright	2. Chris Lawler
3. John Bailey	3. Gerry Byrne
4. Peter Reid	4. Phil Thompson
5. Dave Watson	7. Jimmy Case
6. Brian Labone	8. John Aldridge
7. Colin Harvey	9. Robbie Fowler
8. Paul Bracewell	10. Tommy Smith
9. Joe Royle	11. Ian Callaghan
18. Wayne Rooney	17. Steven Gerrard
60. Dixie Dean	20. Terry McDermott

Subs	Subs
11. Johnny Morrissey	5. Sammy Lee
12. Alan Harper	12. David Fairclough
14. Derek Temple	14. Steve McManaman
15. Terry Darracott	15. Steve McMahon
99. Dave Hickson	16. David Johnson
	23. Jamie Carragher

Key Areas

JA: It's all over to be fair. They have got two lads up front and no wingers, so I'd imagine Reidy would be asking Harvey and Bracewell to get wide going forward.

PR: To be fair, this kid (points at Rooney's name), has got all the ability to get back and move around. Without blowing my own bugle, I think the other lads in midfield are intelligent enough to move where they have to when they need to deal with things.

JA: I don't know whether Rooney is (laughs).

PR: (Laughing) I know Aldo probably thinks we would knock it long, but we don't have the players to play long ball. The two centre-backs can't kick it and I couldn't kick it, so we're not long ball. Bails had a good left foot and he was a great player (points at Tommy Wright), so just keep it away from Watto and Labone and we will try and play through them.

JA: I would ask our centre-backs to take either Royle or Dean, because they both offer the same threat. You couldn't just say 'you mark him and you mark him', because of the movement.

PR: Unfortunately, none of us here will have seen Dixie, but his record is just ridiculous in

terms of goals; I mean it's frightening. Just that would strike fear. I'd love to have Dave Hickson up there as well. That would be a bruising partnership.

JA: Well have him then on your bench...as long as I can nick Steve McMahon.

PR: McMahon played for Everton first though didn't he?

JA: Alright Reidy, you can't have both of them, let's be fair! (laughter)

PR: F*** Macca off then (draws a cross through his name). I'll get my assistant to tell Macca he's not playing!

Weaknesses

JA: There are some major battles. I'm still worried for Reidy defensively. But they have a great forward line too. Their three would be a match for any side in the world. Brazil would be f****** worried about that. With

'I'd want my players to pressurise Bails and not let him get it on his left foot cos he'd look to bang it in to Dixie Dean or Joe Royle'

Rooney in behind Dean, and Joe being a target man as well, it would be a big job for Tommo, Smithy and obviously Stevie G to check them out. Gerry Byrne and Chris Lawler would have to remember their defensive duties as well.

PR: Our midfield isn't bad too you know?!

JA: Well I would look to exploit your lack of width.

PR: We have the players to deal with that though. Everyone can shuffle over when they have to.

JA: I'm really looking down this right hand side and thinking I am going to be able to get at Bails. I think it could reap dividends with Lawler and Case down there.

PR: I think with Bails' left foot and Tommy Wright and us being narrow in the middle of the park, I would like my full-backs to get forward. We can get crosses in to Dean and Royle and make sure Rooney sits in the hole to pick up the pieces. Rooney playing in the

'Bloody hell, I've left McManaman out of the squad haven't I? I'll add him but I can't leave the likes of McDermott, Case, Cally or Stevie out of the side can I?'

hole and Stevie and Terry Mac naturally wanting to go forward all the time, I think that could be a weakness for them. Maybe not one of their weaknesses, because they are playing 4-4-2 with a nice balance, but I just think it's an area of the pitch that we could exploit.

JA: I disagree. There's no great pace in their forward line.

PR: You're wrong Aldo, because I have been led to believe that Dean was electric. He had pace and lots of it. They reckon he was quick. Brilliant in the air too. It's interesting because I am usually a 4-4-2 man myself, but having looked at my squad and the quality I have got, I have decided to go with that instead and change it. There's a little bit of envy, because Aldo has a nice balance looking at it.

JA: Yeah, It's a great side isn't it?!

PR: But, with Rooney in my side, a player who I think is a great player by the way, and will turn out to be one of the greatest. I mean...

JA: (Interrupting) Bloody hell, I have left McManaman out of the squad haven't I? I forgot about him. I'll add him to my squad, but I can't leave out the likes of McDermott, Case, Cally and Stevie can I? They have won leagues, FA Cups and European Cups while at Liverpool, so it would be unfair to leave any of them out. Steve McManaman was a terrific player. He's on the bench (laughs).

PR: (Laughing) He's got the longest bench in the world! Mind you, Sammy Lee's there, so it wouldn't need to be that long. Cheers Sam. (laughter)

PR: There's a month's curfew before the game by the way. No drinking for a month. That goes on record (laughter). That's to nobody specific, I want us to be fit.

JA: There's no way Bails would be able to go that long without a drink. He'd be having eight the night before, so I'd look to exploit that. I'm not saying he wasn't a good player, because he was, but I'd want my players to pressurise him and not let him get it on his left foot, cos he'd look to bang it in to Dixie Dean or Joe Royle. They'd be looking to hit the front man as early as possible.

PR: It's very difficult to pick weaknesses though isn't it?

JA: You've just hit the nail on the head. I'm only targeting Bails because of the shape of Reidy's team, without having anyone in front of him. There's no curfew on my team by the way. There's no way Terry Mac would be able to last that long! (laughs). We all liked a pint in our day. There was nothing better than going out after a game. We'd all be back at training on Monday, so there wasn't a problem. That's the way it was, but it's changed.

Wembley opens its doors as the countdown to kick-off continues

The ref

PR: Can I ask a question? (Without waiting) On this theme, is the game going to be played today when there's no tackling? If it is, I'm not playing. That kid getting sent off for Chelsea (John Obi Mikel) was a disgrace. For that? I mean, what's going on?
JA: Clive Thomas can referee the game then!
PR: I'm not having Clive Thomas refereeing!! Neil Midgeley was the best referee around. He was a Manc, so at least he would be unbiased I suppose. Joe Worrall was a good referee as well.
JA: Without a doubt, big time yeah. They were both tremendous.
PR: You could give Neil jip, but he would just give it back to you. He refereed with common sense, but that doesn't count these days. He was a big Man City fan.
JA: The fact that we have both said him speaks volumes. If you swore at him, he'd just say things like, 'get on with it you moaning b******' type of thing.
PR: He was top class.

Q: Who would get booked first?

JA: I think Tommy Smith would have to be careful. With Rooney being on the other side, I think he'd be looking to give him a kick early on. He'd be thinking to himself, 'Little Rooney, first chance I get, I'm going to test the water with the referee here.' Because that's the way he was. If he could catch him!
PR: You talk about Tommy being hard, but he was ever so fair too. I can't remember Tommy ever really trying to hurt someone deliberately. He'd go in really hard, but he was fair. He was a top, top player.
JA: That's the great thing about both teams, they are all great footballers, but they can all handle themselves too, so it would be really tough. People might say the likes of Cally are quiet, but he would stand up to anyone if he had to. Colin Harvey had the

same type of temperament for Everton too.

Q: Why do you think Scousers are so tough?

JA: It's the way we are brought up. There's no silver spoon in our mouths.
PR: It comes back to that story when they were building Knowsley Safari Park doesn't it? They had a council meeting and an old lady stood up and said 'what about a lion? What happens if a lion escapes?' A councillor responded, 'It's gonna take it's chances.' (laughter)

Q: What about the TV cameras?

JA: It's a good point. We'd have to be careful what we do.
PR: Right, Johnny Morrissey is coming on then with 20 minutes to go just to stir it up! (laughter)
JA: Well if Johnny is coming on, so must Carragher, because Chris Lawler is a bit too quiet for Johnny, and Carra might be able to stand up to him.
PR: All the best then Carra. He'll love you for that! (laughter)

Goalkeeping problems

JA: The major problem we both have is with the goalkeepers.
PR: I'm quite happy with my one compared to his! (laughter). My one was nicknamed the sheep dog because of his bad haircut.
JA: I would be asking Steve Gerrard, Jimmy Case and Terry Mac to shoot on sight, big time. The goalkeeping situation on both sides would add to the score at the end of the game.
PR: Yeah, there's too many quality players going forward and both sides would find it hard to contain. Especially with these two keepers behind them.
JA: All goalkeepers are nutters and Scousers aren't that f****** soft and that's

why there are so few keepers about. We're too canny; we're too clever to go in goal.
PR: It just shows you that everyone wants to f****** play out doesn't it? If you were in the school yard, you didn't go in goal if you could play.
JA: We were the first ones to introduce 'goalie in-and-out.' That was the Liverpool way. Goalie in and out. First goal, then go out.
PR: That's true. There were no heroes to look up to as well. No Scouse heroes. We've had great goalkeepers at both clubs, but no Scousers.
JA: Yeah, Clemence, Big Nev...
PR: All the fat kids with glasses went in goal when we were in school.

Q: Which outfield player would go in goal in an emergency?

PR: If Andy Rankin got injured, I would ask one man. Big Joe. Without a doubt. I have spoken to him and he told me that he always used to go in goal at Bellefield and save a lot. And obviously, he's got a stature. In fact if he was playing now, you wouldn't get a f****** shot past him! (Aldo snorts with laughter).
JA: I'd have to go in myself. I wouldn't want anyone else to because they're too good. I'd definitely go in myself. Sammy Lee would be last choice. We'd need step ladders.

> 'In an emergency I'd definitely go in (goal) myself. Sammy Lee would be last choice. We'd need step ladders'

Pre-match Preparations

SO THE SCENE IS SET.

It's the first true Merseyside final in history and the whole of Liverpool has descended on Wembley for an afternoon nobody will ever forget.

Wembley has been chosen as the location for this unique match after a special agreement between player/managers John Aldridge and Peter Reid.

In a statement to the press, Aldridge said: "We both agree that Wembley should host the game. It's the only stadium that can befit such an occasion."

The tension around the Everton camp in the days leading up to the match is heightened by the confusion surrounding Dave Hickson's potential inclusion in the squad.

Blues tactician Reid orders a hotline to the bods down at Soho Square to see whether Hickson, who was born in Ellesmere Port, Cheshire, is eligible to play for his Everton Scouse XI.

Aside from overlooking the fact that Hickson could feature in the Liverpool squad if he was allowed to play, Reid also forgets to check on the eligibility of some of the other members in his squad including Heswall's Paul Bracewell.

Unusually though Aldo is championing his inclusion. The fact that Brace featured in four FA Cup finals, losing them all, may have something to do with it.

After numerous stories about how Everton always suffer hard luck, the FA relent on what has been labelled by the press as 'the Hickson enquiry'. But judging by the selection of some of his squad people are wondering whether Reidy's been calling the AA rather than the FA!

Wily player-boss John Aldridge is not soft though, and he swiftly arranges the transfer of Steve McMahon from the opposition.

Sadly for the tough midfielder it's the 1986 FA Cup final all over again, as his late registration means that Aldo is reluctant to change his starting XI, so he takes his place on the substitutes' bench.

Back in the Everton dressing room, everyone's arguing what number shirt they should wear. Hickson (as if he's not caused enough fuss already) politely asks Joe Royle for his number nine jersey. Joe obliges, but this time the FA intervene and say alterations to squad numbers can't be made at this late stage.

In the end, Hickson etches another nine on Royle's spare shirt and becomes the Blues' first ever 99.

Dixie Dean, meanwhile, tries to wind Reds up by reminding them of his goalscoring feat in 1927/28 by wearing the number 60 shirt.

Sadly for Dixie, everyone's too busy being startled by five shining gold stars on the chest of every Liverpool player, symbolising their European Cup victories. Nice try Dixie.

Team talk

PR: I'd just say: "Listen Dixie, Smithy never stops talking as you know, and he says you're not going to have a kick." I rest my case (laughter). Seriously though, they're a quality side and it's important to stop the likes of Gerrard and McDermott shooting and making runs. When you look at Aldo and Fowler and their finishing ability, they're two of the best, so I'd get Brian Labone to make sure the defence stays narrow. Let's use what I think is our strength by getting wide and getting lots of crosses in, and wait for Rooney to do it in the hole. Let him get at them the best he could, and that would be my team talk. I don't think I would need to target players and try to get them wound up, because all the players in the Liverpool side have been there and seen it all and wouldn't be affected by it. You're talking about players who have won things; so you're not going to try and wind the likes of Smithy up are you, or Jimmy Case?

JA: It's a good point that.

PR: Yeah, 'See you after for a bevvie.'

JA: I would just say that I fancy us going forward and to do the right things there. To keep the concentration defensively and all over the park. With Rooney, you know, be aware of him and keep an eye on his movement. Second balls, we must win all the time.

PR: (Interrupting) I'm drinking a blue glass of wine here.

JA: Erm, I'd also tell them to get in their faces. It would be the same from both sides, but f****** hell, who's going to win that battle?

PR: If it becomes a kicking game by the way, I am calling for Johnny Morrissey (laughter).

Looking to the captain

JA: It's been hard picking a captain though hasn't it?

PR: The only thing the captain would do in this team is toss up. I mean, there's so many leaders in the team...

JA: (Interrupting) Tommy Smith for me. He's a leader and wouldn't expect anything but the best. He's the most Scouse of the Scousers too, so deserves it on that basis as well.

PR: Usually, I look to have my captain at the back, but I am looking for inspiration, so Dixie's nearly 400 goals wins it for him. He's got to wear the armband. All the stories when you read about it, I mean people forget what a legend he is just cos he played in the 1920s.

Set-pieces

PR: They reckon that Dean could hit a ball and this kid (points at Rooney) can hit a ball with accuracy, so I'd be looking towards those two.

JA: I'd be concerned with corners against the height of Royle and the ability of Dean, Watto and Labby. That's a big presence in the box. Gerrard would have to come back and use his height.

PR: I'd tell the lads to stay on their feet too, because if we give free-kicks away around the box, you'd have to fancy Jimmy Case or Stevie.

JA: They'd be my men.

PR: Zonal marking then Aldo?

JA: None of that sh*** no, it's too risky marking areas.

In the tunnel

PR: All the stuff that went on in the tunnel. F****** hell, that was part and parcel of it. Let's forget about these days of political correctness. We'd get into each other. There would be plenty at it in this game. I'd pick on Terry Mac cos he's my mate and I'd leave Brace to have a go at Smithy (laughs). Dixie and Smithy would be left to get on with it.

> **'A lot of the lads who are playing against each other grew up in the same districts. The respect would be immense'**

Tommo would probably talk Joe Royle to boredom!

JA: You're talking about Scousers here. We've got too much mental strength on both sides to be fooled around in the tunnel. Everything that's said is like water off a duck's back.

PR: All the players know each other anyway, so there would be competitive banter, but a level of respect too. Whatever you say, it's a massive rivalry between the players, but a huge amount of respect too. There's too much quality on the pitch to get caught up in mind games.

JA: You have to remember that a lot of the lads who are playing against each other grew up in the same districts and have played against each other all of their lives. The respect would be immense. Game on.

(Main) The crowd flock down Wembley Way ahead of the big game while (left) Red Arrows mark the occasion

First half

WITH the whole Everton squad running out onto the pitch five minutes before the bell rings, the genius of Bill Shankly transcends and Aldo orders Gerry Byrne out of the dressing room.

The squad are confused and Gerry looks like he's been given the flick when Aldo follows him out and tells him to walk onto the pitch holding the latest of Liverpool's five European Cups.

Aldo returns to the dressing room and explains the method behind the madness.

"Shanks was a master tactician and performer of mind games which led him to pull off a masterstroke just prior to Liverpool's European Cup semi-final against Inter Milan in 1965," says Aldo.

"On that occasion, he ordered Gerry, along with non-Scouser Gordon Milne, onto the pitch at Anfield just before the game was due to kick off. This seems normal enough, but they were holding the recently acquired FA Cup.

"It sent Anfield into a frenzy, the Italians froze, and the Reds triumphed 3-1."

The remaining players inside the Wembley dressing room feel the stadium rock as Byrne steps out on the pitch and the Everton players stand in bewilderment.

Everton had earlier contemplated trying the same trick, but a single Cup Winners' Cup doesn't hold the same kudos as five European Cups.

Eventually, Tommy Smith leads his team out onto the pitch when John Bailey is picked up on TV cameras transfixed by the Reds captain.

He unwittingly informs the rest of the Everton lads that Smithy must be playing up front as he's wearing the number 10 shirt.

The spirit of Shanks has worked again as Aldo is seen rubbing his hands when he enters the arena.

Most Wembley finals at this point would see the teams greeted by a royal audience.

But because this is an all-Scouse final devoid of royal sentiment, both teams run on and just get on with it.

PR: I can see Bails getting up the field with Liverpool trying to shut him down and knocking a raking cross 18 yards out and Liverpool not having time to spot Dixie running in with his raw 13 stone.

Bang, top corner. And Frankie Lane's still singing! (laughter)

JA: Yeah, so what, they may have scored one right at the start, but we're the ones playing the real f****** football! Yeah, they've got a lot of experience through the side, but where are the European Cup winners? We've got loads of them, and our experience tells. My perfect goal would be a lot of players involved in the midfield, out to Cally who puts it on his right foot where I have pulled off Watson and Labone and laid it up for Robbie, who's run in a side-foot volley from six yards. Goal. I haven't scored yet, but I don't care. I wouldn't really celebrate even if I did though. We didn't do that in our day. All that rehearsed running over and punching the corner-flag sh***.

PR: Aldo was worried about his ability to defend set-plays, and he was right because we've just scored from a corner. We've all piled in, and I know John is keen on zonal marking, so we've exploited the space and the corner's gone short to Rooney on the edge of the box for the volley from Colin Harvey's pass. Rooney's volleyed it from 25 yards right in the top corner and Frankie Lane's just stood there and watched it.

JA: There's no way we're going in behind at the break, so I tell Lawler and Case to double up on Bails. This time, Chris Lawler's overlapped, while Bails has gone asleep slightly for a second because he's seen a fella in the crowd with a can of lager! Reidy's pre-match preparations have obviously failed. Chris goes past him and pings a ball far post. Again, I have peeled off Watto, nodded it back to the edge of the box and Stevie G's come in like a steam train and f****** smacked one in the bottom corner. It'd be right on half-time, so it's a sickener for Everton.

> 'Stevie G's come in like a steam train and smacked one in the bottom corner'

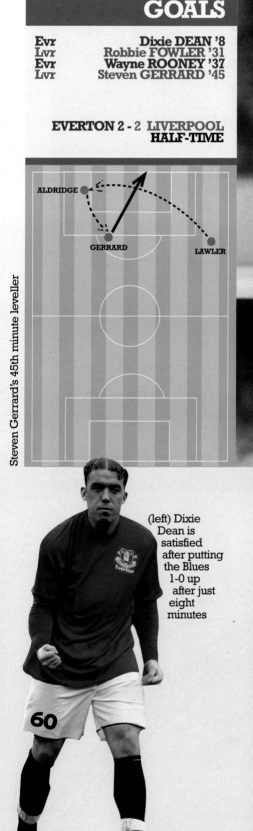

GOALS

Evr	Dixie DEAN '8
Lvr	Robbie FOWLER '31
Evr	Wayne ROONEY '37
Lvr	Steven GERRARD '45

EVERTON 2 - 2 LIVERPOOL
HALF-TIME

ALDRIDGE

GERRARD   LAWLER

Steven Gerrard's 45th minute leveller

(left) Dixie Dean is satisfied after putting the Blues 1-0 up after just eight minutes

(Left) The Liverpool team huddle before the kick-off.
(Below) Gerrard's equaliser on the stroke of half-time was a real sickener for Everton and changed Peter Reid's team talk

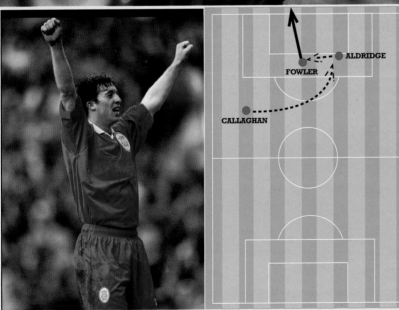

Robbie Fowler is on form, and his strike is a typical poacher's goal

The second half >

The fanatical support inside Wembley eagerly await the second half

'They didn't expect him to get forward, but there he is, the ghost himself, Chris Lawler'

NEIL MIDGELEY blows his whistle for half-time and the Evertonians are going spare.

Preferring to blame bad luck for conceding a goal just before the break, they can't see that the equaliser was their own fault because of a lack of concentration.

The Liverpool players do the professional thing meanwhile. They may have scored late on in the first half, but they understand the game is yet to be won.

Captain Tommy Smith puts things in perspective by keeping each player on his toes with a stinging back slap as they walk off.

The players trudge down the tunnel and into the dressing rooms where the managers have different messages for their sides.

PR: I'm sorry, but Watto and Labby are going to be told off. They're going to have some stick. Aldo's pulled off them twice. 'What have I told you before Watto and Labby, they've got quality in their movement and you can't let Aldo get on your shoulder like that.' That's what I'd say!

JA: I'd be like, 'Well lads, we can't give too many corners away, get your leg round it and put it up the pitch or out for throw-ins. Just don't give it away for a corner.'

Q. What's the atmosphere like at the break?

PR: It's electric, Wembley's never seen anything like it. When you've got fanatical support like you do in the city, atmosphere ain't a problem. With these players on show, you're talking about the best of Merseyside here, so it would take some beating.

JA: Yeah, the players are knocking the s*** out of each other fairly, then dusting themselves down and getting on with it. Not like these Chelsea players of today and the Ronaldos going to ground.

Second half

PR: We finally get some joy through the middle of the park and Rooney breaks free. Tommo has to come out to stop him, but Rooney plays a one-two with Dixie and plays him in. Then Tommy Smith comes in with a great flying challenge. Luckily for me, I have got up with play for once and the ball rebounds against my face, over Frankie Lane's head and into the open net. I'm absolutely delighted because it's a fluke.

JA: My choice of Chris Lawler is vindicated because there's a great six-man build-up with Cally, Gerry Byrne, Robbie and Steve Gerrard involved. I have made a near post run, which has taken the two centre-backs

away from the back post – they didn't listen to Reidy at half-time. They didn't expect him to get forward, but there he is, the ghost himself, Chris Lawler, volley, through the f****** goalkeeper's legs. Poor old Rankin.

PR: I'm not having this. Aldo, you've been involved in all the goals and Watto and Labby are having a nightmare. The goalie's had a mare (laughter).

JA: So quickly, there's a fourth goal! Robbie gets involved in the midfield. Six or seven passes and Jimmy Case blasts it from 30 yards. For once, goalkeeper Rankin pulls off a f****** worldie, but there I am all on my own at the back post – just pulled off Watto (laughs) – I tap it in.

PR: At this point, I would usually like to keep my back four the same shape, but Bails is off and Johnny Morrissey is on cos we need a physical presence in there. We've got some great subs like Alan Harper, who's brilliant, Derek Temple, tremendous, Davie Hickson, but it's Morrissey who I choose. I say, 'Come on Bails, you've had a great game, but come off son, the centre-halves have let you down badly.' It pays dividends because with the clock ticking, Johnny hoists a ball into the box and Dixie goes elbows and beats Tommy Smith to the ball. It whistles past Frankie and he's still singing!

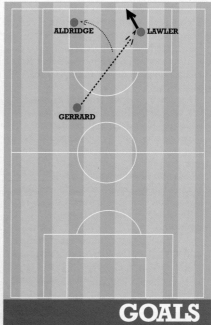

(Below) Chris Lawler's 74th minute strike

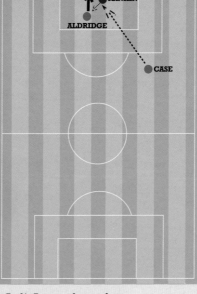

(Left) A turn of pace from Aldridge gives him the space to slot home Liverpool's fourth

GOALS

Evr	Dixie **DEAN** '8
Lvr	Robbie **FOWLER** '31
Evr	Wayne **ROONEY** '37
Lvr	Steven **GERRARD** '45

second half

Evr	Peter **REID** '61
Lvr	Chris **LAWLER** '74
Lvr	John **ALDRIDGE** '76
Evr	Dixie **DEAN** '87

EVERTON 4 - 4 LIVERPOOL
After 87 minutes

THE NEAREST THING TO A SCOUSE FINAL

AHEAD of the Milk Cup Final on March 25 1984, Stan Flashman made a predictable observation.

"I expect the price of tickets will be good on the black market. Personally, I would charge double the face value," said London's best loved/loathed ticket tout.

Given the extreme lengths that Scousers go to to watch their teams, he was probably right.

Black market tradesmen must have rejoiced at the sight of more than 100,000 Scousers bouncing up Wembley Way.

The Milk Cup final provided the closest match we've ever had to a true Scouse – or at least Merseyside – final.

The squads may not have been filled with Scousers, but the sense of unity amongst both sets of players and supporters created 'Merseypride.'

Local passions were at their peak during a time when the city was in a state of despair.

In an era of unemployment, deteriorating housing conditions and riots, the city's only comfort was in its football teams.

The grave situation reached its nadir when church leaders offered special prayers for the city on budget day.

In adversity, the city united and Liverpool vs Everton filled Scousers with pride.

Reds and Blues travelled south together. Special all-Merseyside coaches were laid on as fans joined together for a chorus of 'Merseyside, Merseyside, Merseyside.'

Like most games of utmost importance, the final ended up being an anti-climax, and only a Graeme Souness goal in the replay at Maine Road ended up separating the teams.

> '**Fairclough's run onto it exactly the same as St Etienne and placed it calmly underneath Rankin. The celebration's the same too**'

(Right) Fairclough is elated by scoring the winner, as are the Liverpool fans (left)

GOALS

	first half	
Evr	**Dixie DEAN** '8	
Lvr	**Robbie FOWLER** '31	
Evr	**Wayne ROONEY** '37	
Lvr	**Steven GERRARD** '45	

	second half	
Evr	**Peter REID** '61	
Lvr	**Chris LAWLER** '74	
Lvr	**Jimmy CASE** '76	
Evr	**Dixie DEAN** '87	
Lvr	**David FAIRCLOUGH** '90	

EVERTON 4 - 5 LIVERPOOL
FULL TIME

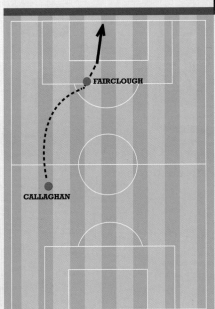

FAIRCLOUGH

CALLAGHAN

The winning goal

MOST teams at this point would crumble after conceding such a late equaliser. But not Liverpool.

The Reds have won more league titles and European Cups than any other club in England because of their expertise in tight pressure moments.

Aldo thinks what Shanks would do in this situation and quickly orders Smithy to kick off. Not from the centre circle, but on a player!

At key points in games, the great man would order Smithy to start a fight, thus breaking the opposition's concentration.

Before you can say 'We've won it five times' Smithy is trading haymakers with Wayne Rooney and both squads pile in.

Meanwhile, Steve McMahon is still grumbling on the bench and desperate to get on, especially since he appeared prominently on the squad's pre-match song as Brian Moore said: 'Steve McMahon

sure can rap, it's about time he had a Scousers cap.'

Moore's murmurings go unheard as Aldo calls for Supersub instead.

JA: It's a tough one, but I bring myself off and bring Davie Fairclough on. It's like St Etienne all over again. I'll never forget that game until the day I die, and there he is, Fairclough does it again! It's exactly the same again. He runs onto a long ball and he gets in between Labone and Watson (laughs)...

PR: (laughing) I knew you were going to say that!

JA: He's run onto it exactly the same and placed it calmly underneath Rankin. The celebration's the same too. The famous jump and everything.

Reds boss Aldridge: I just told Davie 'Grab us a winner and the drinks are on me' — Page 41

SUPERSUB STRIKES TO STEAL DERBY THRILLER

Wembley joy for Reds as Fairclough repeats St Etienne trick to leave rivals feeling blue

DAVID FAIRCLOUGH is the toast of Anfield once again after his dramatic late goal sealed victory for Liverpool in the all-Scouse Merseyside derby at Wembley

A packed house at the country's national stadium saw a fantastic match with all of the best talent ever to represent Merseyside on show to thrill an ecstatic crowd

The friendly atmosphere off the pitch was only rivalled by the entertainment on it with both sides locked at 4-4 going into the final moments

T at was the moment history repeated itself for the Reds when Fairclough, who had only been on the pitch a few minutes, raced clear and slotted the ball under Andy Rankin for the crucial goal – just as he had done against St Etienne all those years ago

Full match report and reaction on Pages 42-47

BY STANLEY PARK

It was the perfect ending for John Aldridge's Liverpool side at the end of a topsy-turvy match

Robbie Fowler, Steven Gerrard, Chris Lawler and Aldridge had given the Reds a 4-3 lead but Dixie Dean drew the scores level with only a few minutes to spare to add to his earlier effort and goals from Wayne Rooney and Everton manager Peter Reid

With Dave Watson and Brian Labone tiring at the back Fairclough took full advantage to send the Liverpool fans delirious

Liverpool FC's Scouse XI manager Aldridge said "I'm delighted We'll crack open a few tins on the coach back to Liverpool and try and keep the party going for days"

The Liverpool ECHO is printed by Trinity Mirror and is registered at the Post Office and more words along here that most people don't ready anyway and doesn't really matter what words are written prop deck

The back page of the Liverpool ECHO delivers news and reaction after David Fairclough's late Wembley winner

TERRY MAC'S CONTROL LETS HIM DOWN

AFTER lifting the European Cup in 1977, the Liverpool squad returned to the city in a party mood.

Like every good Scouser, Terry McDermott enjoyed a few drinks.

Phil Thompson reveals what happened next:

"There is the legendary story of Terry, out of his mind after a famous city centre European Cup trophy parade in 1977, peeing over the balcony onto some unsuspecting first aid girls down below. Of course, he didn't know anyone was down there. I was standing next to him, but couldn't do anything about it.

"The next day he said to me 'Tell me I was not having a pee over the balcony.' When he realised it had happened he said, 'You are joking.' He couldn't remember.

"Terry was an unbelievable character. The lads nicknamed him "Lege" which was short for "Legend".

"He was such a bubbly and funny character and helped to make the dressing room light-hearted and relaxed. He was like that from the day he came. I should say that he had a strange sense of humour.

"Terry could drink and get home at two in the morning, but he could still get through any fitness regime you could throw at him the next day. That was never a problem for him. He could go in a sauna for 20 minutes without breaking sweat! He actually hated the sauna. I remember he had a chain that he wore round his neck. I can remember him being in the sauna and the chain must have been getting hotter and hotter. He suddenly screamed in pain. It was really funny."

Aldo knows the celebrations after his Liverpool FC Scouse XI's victory would have been almost as legendary as the match itself

Post match

FOR LIVERPOOL Wembley has been a suitably grandiose setting for one of their greatest nights, with Fairclough's late strike a fitting winner.

For Everton, not for the first time in their history, optimism has turned to self-pity as they again manage to keep up their time honoured tradition of stealing defeat from the jaws of glory (well, at least a glorious draw).

Both squads travel home separately, but meet up in Aldo's bar later on for a cocktail or two.

In true Scouse fashion, Smithy and Wazza Rooney forget about their differences on the pitch and share a pina colada at the bar.

JA: The cans are out. Champagne, I'm not too keen on that, but there would be a few bottles flying around. Lots of Guinness and bitter. We get the coach on the way back, full of ale. Terry McDermott's organised everything and we're all back to Aldo's Place. Never to be f****** seen again. Half-past ten, I'd give Reidy a call and tell him to get the lads over cos it's a three-day bender.

'Half-past ten I'd give Reidy a call and tell him to get the lads over cos it's a three-day bender'

Gary ABLETT

Dave HICKSON

David JOHNSON

CROSSING STANLEY PARK

Playing for both Liverpool AND Everton might seem a tricky proposition, but the two clubs have completed the most direct transfers between British sides in history. We take a look at the players that have crossed the Mersey divide

WHILE the whole world concentrated on the antics of the USSR and the West during the uncertain years following WWII, Merseyside was experiencing a Cold War of its own.

Liverpool City Council may not have been conducting Berlin-style airlifts or erecting Checkpoint Charlies on the gates of Stanley Park, but the lack of transfer activity formed a frosty front and few players crossed the border between the city's two teams for more than 40 years.

Liverpool did not buy a player directly from Everton between 1959 and 2000, while there was a similar freeze in the other direction from 1961 until 1982.

Unparalleled success for both sides during this period may have something to do with the stand-off.

Bearing this in mind, it is quite surprising to find that during the course of history, Liverpool and Everton have completed more direct transfers between each other than any other clubs in Britain.

Equally surprising is the fact that Scousers haven't been afraid to cross the divide.

Despite the intense local rivalry, it didn't stop players like David Johnson becoming the only Scouse player to score in a red and a blue shirt in a Merseyside derby.

Similarly, the only Scouser to have captained both sides is Steve McMahon.

We look at some of the Scouse players to have made an impact while wearing either red or blue.

Dave Hickson

Playing career 1948-64
Everton Apps (goals) 243 (111)
Liverpool Apps (goals) 67 (38)

HICKSON was the first true legend from either Liverpool or Everton to bridge the Mersey divide.

Numerous players had represented both clubs before him, but the striker, who was labelled the Cannonball Kid by the Gwladys Street, caused uproar when he moved in 1959.

Just as much as Evertonians treasured him, Liverpudlians disliked him, so when he signed on at Anfield some Kopites were so incensed that they threatened to tear up their season tickets.

A day later, all was forgotten as he grabbed both goals in a 2-1 win over Aston Villa, ironically another of his former clubs.

Earlier in his career, Evertonians lauded Hickson as he provided an enigmatic brew of undeniable devotion, fighting spirit (with opposition players and sometimes even referees), and most of all goals.

Hickson also has the distinction of playing for Tranmere Rovers, being the only player to appear for all three Merseyside clubs.

David Johnson

Playing career 1969-85
Liverpool Apps (goals) 217 (78)
Everton Apps (goals) 105 (20)

DAVID Johnson's career followed a curious path.

After making a goalscoring debut for Everton in the FA Youth Cup, Central League, Football League, FA Cup, League Cup and in Europe, he eventually moved to Ipswich.

A decent goalscoring spell in Suffolk (where he also scored on his debut) was followed by a return to Merseyside with Liverpool under Bob Paisley.

Johnson failed to net in his first game, but went on to be a prominent figure in arguably Liverpool's greatest ever side between 1978 and 1980.

The striker then crossed Stanley Park again, signing for Everton in 1983, where he struggled for form, before spells in America and Malta.

Ablett played in FA Cup finals for both Everton and Liverpool

Gary Ablett

Playing career 1986-2001
Liverpool Apps (goals) 147 (1)
Everton Apps (goals) 156 (6)

GARY Ablett became one of the first victims of a major squad overhaul undertaken by Graeme Souness in 1992.

But the move eventually enabled him to become the only player to have won the FA Cup with both Liverpool and Everton.

Ablett featured in the Liverpool side that defeated Everton in 1989 – a year after losing to Wimbledon – before winning the same trophy with the Blues in 1995.

A versatile defender, Ablett played at left-back and centre-back in a red shirt, before filling the same roles while wearing blue.

He moved across Stanley Park again in 2006 when he left Everton's Academy for a role as Liverpool's reserve team coach, thus making him the only player to have left Liverpool for Everton directly, before returning to Anfield again.

Other Scousers who have represented Everton and Liverpool

Ben Howard Baker, John Whitehead, Arthur Berry, Ted Harthill, Jack Heydon, Tony McNamara, Johnny Morrissey, Dave Watson

Steve McMAHON

Robbie FOWLER

Peter REID

SWITCHING SIDES

Changing allegiance to your club's derby rivals normally makes you the subject of contempt, but some players are so good they make you forget the past

IN OTHER football-gripped cities across the world supporters are divided by one of five sacred factors.

Usually it is history, politics, class, religion or geography that separates footy nuts, yet it is worth remembering that they are not all mutually exclusive.

In Liverpool, for some reason, rivalry between the city's two sets of fans doesn't include any symbolic dynamics or follow any logical pattern.

Maybe this makes it slightly easier for boyhood Blues to grow up to become Reds legends, or indeed, the other way around.

That is not saying that the rivalry is any less intense than in other cities, but there is no escaping the fact that there have been many players over the years to grow up supporting one team, before making their names with the other.

Here are just a few of them.

Jamie CARRAGHER

Jamie Carragher

Grew up supporting EVERTON
Became LIVERPOOL LEGEND

JAMIE Carragher doesn't score many goals, so the only time we get to see him celebrate is when Liverpool win a major trophy, or indeed a derby match.

Given the way Carragher rejoiced after a late strike secured Liverpool's victory at Goodison Park in October 2007, it is hard to believe that he ever stood on the Gwladys Street as a kid.

Carragher and former Reds right-back Stephen Wright were spotted by Liverpool scouts at an early age playing for their district side and, unlike other players, didn't really attracted too much attention from Everton.

> '**When you're a young lad, your favourite players change every week. I loved Graeme Sharp, then it was Peter Reid, then it was Gary Lineker'**
>
> **- Carra on his loyalties as a youngster**

He's been at Melwood pretty much ever since and despite hailing from a staunch Everton background, his achievements in a red shirt have led most of his family to follow the Reds.

"My whole family were mad Evertonians, but now we're red through and through.

"You can't afford to be in both camps if you live in this city and I am, and always will be, a Red."

Steve McMahon

Grew up supporting EVERTON
Became LIVERPOOL LEGEND

A FORMER Everton ball boy, McMahon didn't want to risk the wrath of Blues fans by leaving his boyhood club for Anfield directly, so instead he signed for Aston Villa upon leaving Goodison Park in 1983.

Within two years though, he'd moved back to Merseyside when Kenny Dalglish made him his first signing after taking charge of the Reds.

The only Scouser to have captained both clubs, McMahon loathed Liverpool as a youngster.

But it didn't stop him becoming a legend across Stanley Park as the tough, hard working midfielder became the perfect complement to flair players like John Barnes and Jan Molby.

"I suppose it's inevitable to wonder what might have happened if I had gone to Liverpool. They won three trophies last season while Villa had a difficult time. But you have to make the decision at the time, and I felt that going across Merseyside was the hardest move in football."

– McMahon on his initial decision to reject Liverpool

Robbie Fowler

Grew up supporting EVERTON
Became LIVERPOOL LEGEND

GOD, as Kopites came to call him, was, in his own words, 'Everton daft' as a kid.

He grew up as a rabid Blue and openly admits that as a youngster the best night of his life was watching his heroes beat Bayern Munich in the European Cup Winners Cup in 1985.

Yet when both Merseyside clubs came calling for his signature, it was Liverpool he chose.

Fowler went on trial at Bellefield, impressed and the Blues were desperate to sign him.

Despite the best efforts of Stuart McCall, who Fowler says made a real fuss of him on a visit to Goodison Park, the Toxteth-born striker decided to go to Melwood after persistence from Kenny Dalglish.

183 goals later in a red shirt, Fowler became a true legend at Anfield.

Evertonians hated him in equal measure as he often saved his best performances for games against the Blues.

Dubious goal celebrations over the years didn't help either!

> 'In many ways, the phenomenon that surrounded me was even bigger than the stuff Wayne Rooney gets now...and the Everton fans really f****** despised that'
>
> **– Fowler on Evertonians**

Peter Reid

Grew up supporting LIVERPOOL
Became EVERTON LEGEND

REID stood on the Kop as a boy, cheering on the great Liverpool sides of the late 60s and early 70s.

But now his loyalties lie firmly with Everton after becoming a driving force in arguably their greatest ever side in the mid-80s.

"My family were Reds and, for my sins, so was I. They played great football when I watched them and it was easy to support them.

> "Now though, I am a Blue and nothing will ever change that."
>
> **– Reid on where his loyalties lie**

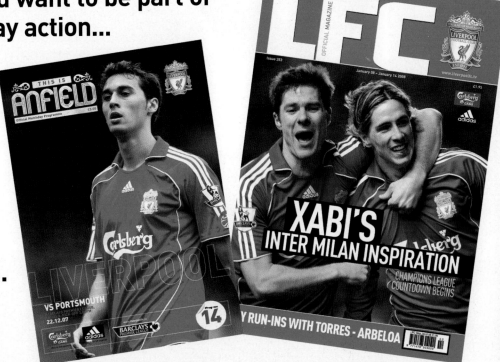

EARLY SCOUSERS

FOOTBALL historians sometimes overlook the achievements of players that plied their trade in the pre and inter war years. Here's our tribute to the Scouse greats that time almost forgot

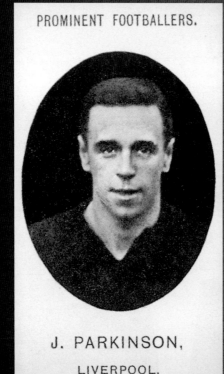

PROMINENT FOOTBALLERS.

J. PARKINSON,

LIVERPOOL.

Jack Parkinson
Striker

D.O.B 13/09/1883 (died 1942)
Liverpool Career Apps 220 (1903-1914)
Goals 130

YOU only have to look at Jack Parkinson's goalscoring ratio to understand that he was the first great Scouse striker to don a Liverpool shirt.

At the age of 20 he netted 21 goals in just 23 league and cup fixtures as the Reds powered towards the Second Division championship.

A year later, despite missing a large portion of the campaign through injury, he scored five goals in a single game against Middlesbrough in mid-March.

Then another six goals before the end of the season steered Liverpool towards the First Division title.

Despite the team stalking mediocrity for the rest of his Anfield career, it is no surprise that in the only other decent season they had (finishing second), Parkinson scored 30 league goals.

Tom Bromilow
Left-half

D.O.B 10/10/1894 (died 1959)
Liverpool Career Apps 375 (1919-29)
Goals 11

DEMOBILISED from the army after the First World War, Tom Bromilow turned up at Anfield one afternoon in 1919 asking for a trial.

Manager George Patterson was impressed, signed him up, and within four years Liverpool had won back-to-back First Division championships for the first time in their history.

This feat was in no small part down to the influence of Bromilow, who was an inspirational leader on and off the pitch.

Walter Wadsworth
Centre-back

D.O.B 07/10/1890 (died 1951)
Liverpool Career Apps 241 (1915-26)
Goals 8

WHEN Walter Wadsworth made his Liverpool debut against Middlesbrough on March 20, 1915, it is unlikely he thought that he would have to wait nearly four years for his next outing.

The Great War interrupted most people's lives and Wadsworth was no different.

But when the world returned to normality, the uncompromising centre-half made up for lost time and was a virtual ever present for the next five years.

Adolf HANSON

Adolf Hanson
Winger

D.O.B 27/07/1912 (died in 1993)
Liverpool Career Apps 177 (1931-38)
Goals 52

DURING the time Hitler's armies were frog-marching across Europe, another Adolf a little closer to home was terrorising defenders across the land.

While Hitler dreamt of conquering Blighty, our Adolf, or Alf as he liked to be called, was doing exactly that, ironically from the left wing position.

After scoring in his second game in a 3-1 loss at home to Middlesbrough, Bootle-born Hanson cemented his place in the Liverpool team by netting again in the memorable 7-4 derby victory over Everton in February 1933.

Despite not featuring in Liverpool's greatest sides, Hanson's goalscoring record of almost one in every three matches gave a threat to opposition full-backs that is often lacking in today's football.

(Top) Alf Hanson finds the net against Wolves in 1933 while (above) he shakes hands with his brother as both men skippered their sides when the Reds met Bolton in 1938

Other pre-war greats Eddie Spicer, Thomas Lucas, Johnny Wheeler

From Kolding to the Kop

to the

Jan Molby inter view

He spent over a decade at Anfield and by the time he
left the club in the mid-1990s his accent was more
Dingle than Denmark. **SIMON HUGHES** finds out what
it means to Jan Molby to be an honorary Scouser.

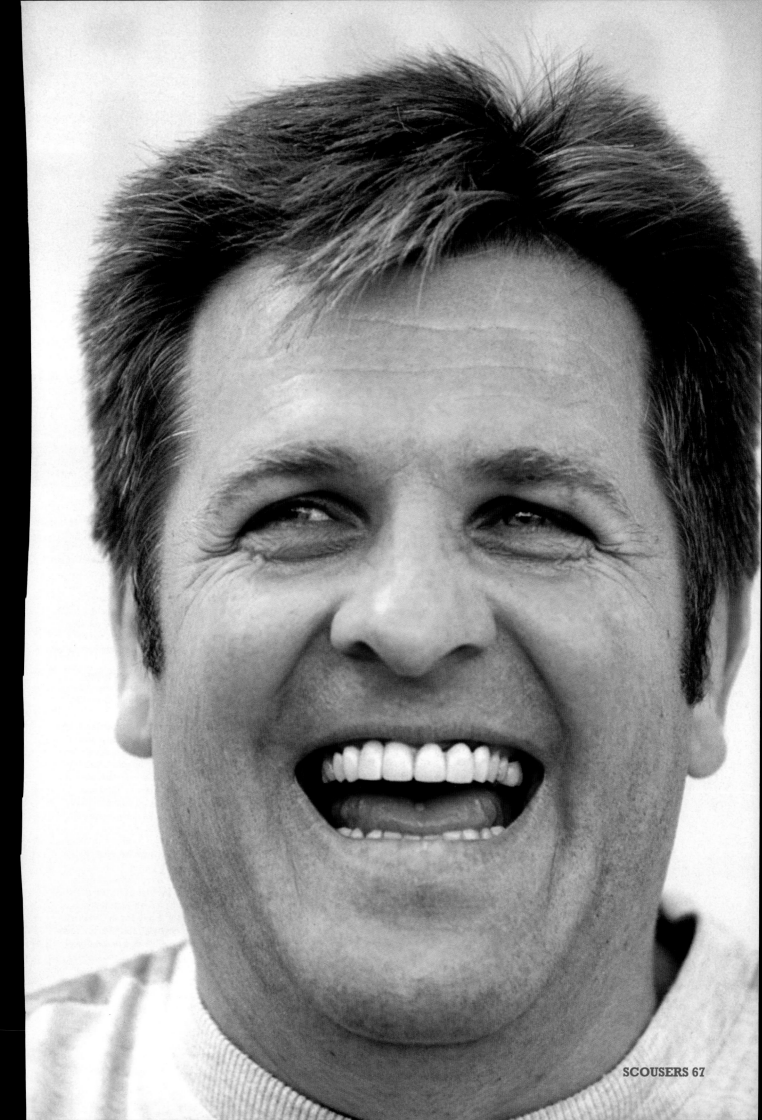

Jan Mølby interview

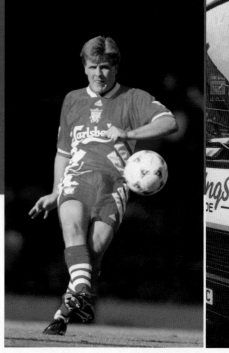

(Far right) **Jan Molby** made such an impact on Merseyside a bus full of his friends and his wife's family made a trip to Denmark for the couple's wedding

JAN MOLBY had only been in Liverpool for less than 24 hours, but there were signs that his life, as he knew it, was about to change.

On a 10-day trial from Ajax, the Dane had completed his first training session at Melwood before returning to a city centre hotel for something to eat and an early night.

Then there was a knock on the door.

"Bruce Grobbelaar was standing there with a smile on his face," explains Molby.

"He was staying at the same place as me and was like, 'right we're going out for a drink.' It all started then. I knew things would be a little different from then on."

A few evenings frequenting city centre nightspots with Grobbelaar and other team members didn't affect Molby during his trial and Joe Fagan decided to sign him soon after.

Molby admits everything was very different to Amsterdam and Denmark – especially the social interaction between players.

"I remember at Ajax once we had a golf day. Johan Cruyff had invited Seve Ballesteros and we all met up at four o'clock in the afternoon. I was set for a big night out, but by seven there were only two players left. That was Jesper Olsen and me, two Danes. It was so different at Liverpool. There were a few all-nighters."

Despite the dissimilarities, Molby didn't find it especially hard settling in and he soon realised why – the genuine nature of Scousers.

"Instantly I felt at home as soon as I signed because the people were so great. That's what makes the city what it is.

"It might not have been a vibrant city at the time because of its economy and the problems it had in the 80s, but everything else was going well in terms of the music scene, the comedy scene and of course the football.

"I realised straight away that at the root of all this was the people. They made the place. The fact that everyone enjoyed a good time too rubbed off on the players who aren't from Liverpool, so we were out and about all the time."

Molby may have felt comfortable straight away, but nothing quite prepared him for his first Merseyside derby.

"You always think you know what it's going to be like don't you? You think that wherever you come from is a football-mad town or city. But nothing compares to Liverpool and what it means to the city. I realised that pretty early on. I hadn't played against Liverpool or Everton, but I had just watched them, so I had an idea what the crowd and the overall support was like. But nothing could prepare me for the reality."

Despite being involved in games between Ajax and Feyenoord, the legendary Dutch derby didn't have the same build-up.

"You always remember your first derby. For me it was the Graeme Sharp goal in 1984, so it wasn't a good one. People had talked so much about the game and the build-up was the whole week because it stretched from Saturday to Saturday.

"People didn't shut up about it. They were saying that it was going to be 100 miles an hour and that it was so competitive. I was like 'yeah, I can handle this,' but really it was worse than that. It was manic. It was a battle."

Molby soon got used to the frenetic nature of the derby, just as he did the stick he used to receive from Evertonians.

"I got caught in a gay bar in Chester in 1987. The next derby all the Evertonians were singing 'Jan Molby's a homosexual.' It was all totally innocent as me and a couple of mates just walked in to a random bar. Before it was too late though, people had snapped us. Nightmare.

"The banter with Evertonians has always been good natured though. I have been led to believe that they put in a bid

> ## 'Scousers seem detached from the rest of England. They live in Scouseland and see themselves as a different breed'

for me once, and I know a lot of Blues were happy with that, so I haven't got a problem with Everton at all."

Everton have not been the only club to be linked with Molby. In 1990 Barcelona were interested. Molby says it was the only time he came close to leaving Liverpool.

"As a player when you're linked away, it doesn't do your ego any harm because it shows you are doing well. Apparently Ronald Koeman had got injured and was going to be out for the whole season. Johan Cruyff had seen me at Ajax and asked his assistant at Barca to draw up a list of players who could replace Koeman. I was on that list and Cruyff said he wanted me. They wanted me to play sweeper and I was quite excited about it.

"At that time, Barcelona won everything in Spain as well as a European Cup, so it would have been a good move. In the end though they didn't sign anyone.

"If I had gone to Barcelona in 1990 and stayed there for four years, I wouldn't be living in Liverpool with my family today. I could have been anywhere in the world, but I am not convinced I would have returned to

Liverpool. I love it here, so that is more important."

Seventeen years on, Molby still resides in the area. Even during his spells managing Swansea, Kidderminster and Hull, he remained at his Wirral home.

Now viewed as an honorary Scouser by people from Liverpool, as well as in his homeland, the big Dane is perfectly placed to sum up people from his adopted city.

"I think Scousers seem detached from the rest of England. They live in Scouseland and I think they see themselves as a different breed to anyone else. But the perception of what Scousers are like and what Liverpool is all about is changing. Years ago, Scousers were the best in the country at poking fun at themselves and they carried that for too long because outsiders actually believed in this false image of the city. It was something made up out of convenience and maybe the comedy scene had something to do with that.

"I have a lot to do with Scandinavians and Germans who come over here and they are all overwhelmed by Scouse people. There can't be any bigger tribute than that. You can go to another city and say things like, 'oh the weather was nice blah blah blah,' but people come to Liverpool and say what a great city it is and how passionate the people are.

"That means a lot more for me than anything. People forget that so many players stay here once they've retired. Alan Hansen, Kenny Dalglish, Mark Wright and Michael Thomas all still live up here. They're all ex-Liverpool players, but came from somewhere else, so there's obviously a reason for that. People love the area."

BEST OF SCOUSE

We ask Jan to rate the Scousers in the Liverpool dressing room

Best Scouse player

"It would have to be Steve McMahon. I think Steve was very much underrated, although that is probably not the right word. He was a much better player than people give him credit for. Yes he was competitive, but he could play and score goals. I loved playing with him and he gave me the platform to go and do what I had to do."

Funniest Scouser

"Aldo. He's a proper 'calm down, calm down' Scouser. He was always on the front foot and aggressive with his humour. He was full of it, telling jokes and gags and he laughed the loudest too. He wasn't so much of a practical joker though. That was left to the Scottish boys like Alan Hansen. Aldo was just in your face.

"We were in a place in Stockholm during pre-season and me and Aldo went for something to eat, just the two of us. The chef in the kitchen kept on looking towards him, looking away then looking again. He obviously thought he knew who he was, so he opened up his top and underneath he had a Juventus shirt. Aldo goes, 'here we go, he thinks I am Ian Rush.' The guy came out and he was going 'Rush, Rush, Rush, Rush.' Aldo was arguing with the fella for about 20 minutes, going 'I am John Aldridge, I'm not Ian f*****g Rush.' The fella wanted his picture taken with him and he was getting offended and he wouldn't have it any other way. I was like, 'come on Rushy, we'll get some free food'!"

Scouse party animal

"It's probably going to be Fowler. Although he was generally a fairly quiet lad, especially at the start, he would come alive at night. He enjoyed a night out in his younger days. Even if we were playing pool or darts, but especially at the Christmas parties. They were legendary. I have been to 12 of them."

Streetwise Scouser

"Sammy Lee was a fully fledged Scouser. Sammy's 'friends' used to come up to the training ground and do little bits and bobs. He would always be asking who's got money on them. Then he'd open the boot on the back of his car and have a load of suits. John Durnin didn't quite make the big time, but he was a proper ducker and diver too."

Plastic Scouser

"Late on, Neil Ruddock was probably the closest player who would put on a bit of an act to try and fit in. Neil's that type of character and would probably like people to see him as a bit of a Scouser."

David FAIRCLOUGH

FCL FUSSBALL CLUB LUZERN

TORONTO FC

LPL

At home with the
Hitzfelds

MOST Scousers that emigrate choose a warm destination. Footballers especially. However, instead of winding down his career in Spain or LA, **David Fairclough** embarked on a continent-hopping trip around the world. And whether he was mixing with European Cup winning managers or World Cup winners, there seemed to be a Scouse influence wherever he went

FOOTBALLERS usually mix in the same circles and reside on the same luxury estates, but it should come as some surprise that David Fairclough was once a neighbour to Ottmar Hitzfeld.

Supersub moved next to the well known Bayern Munich manager while playing in Switzerland for FC Lucerne in 1984.

Hitzfeld had just begun a managerial career with local Second Division side FC Zug, but Fairclough had no idea he would be living close to a man who would eventually go on to become a two-time European Cup winner.

"Ottmar was a really nice bloke. We got to know each other really well over the two years but, of course, I had no idea what was in store for him during his managerial career," recalls Fairclough. "Ottmar's not soft. He was a very hard and organised coach, a typical German really."

Ironically, Lucerne decided to sign the

Anfield born striker as a direct replacement for Hitzfeld, who had decided to take semi-retirement.

"We didn't really talk about the fact that I was his replacement because he was more focused on the coaching at that time. The only time we nearly fell out was when I scored two for Lucerne in a cup match against his side. I suppose it wasn't a very good idea for neighbourly relations."

Fairclough should have known better as it wasn't his first experience of learning to live with foreigners nextdoor.

Two years earlier he had spent the summer in Canada. The move came after Bob Paisley encouraged him to sign for Toronto Blizzard in an attempt to keep up his fitness ahead of the English season.

"It was a great experience and it was the first time I had really stood on my own two feet, even though I was 25. I had a girlfriend who lived back home, but luckily she had a gran who'd moved to Toronto, so she helped me settle in. It was a weird twist of fate really."

Although he soon settled into the Canadian way of life, it was still Scousers who made him feel at home.

"Everywhere you go, there's always a Scouser. And Scousers tend to make themselves heard. They hunted me down wherever I went, especially in Canada.

"It's not just Scousers; it's anyone with Liverpool connections. I'm not sure whether this happens with people from other cities in Britain, but Scousers are really proud and like to look after one another. There was a young lad in the Toronto team who had an aunt from Liverpool and he just couldn't wait to tell me."

The only thing Fairclough found

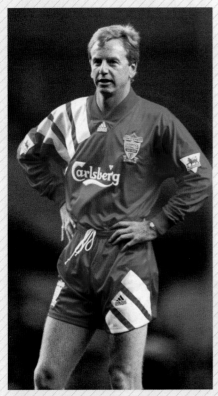

unsettling was the standard of some of the pitches.

"In Chicago, the pitch was half a baseball track and half grass. Our pitch was poor Astroturf. The best pitch was in New York. That ground brought my best memory because Cosmos had Giorgio Chinaglia and Johan Neeskens and Carlos Alberto. We beat them four or five-one on their home patch."

After returning to Liverpool for one season, Fairclough made only eight appearances for the Reds in the league (five from the bench) and decided to finally leave Anfield.

Despite a strong offer from Hannover, Fairclough was put off by the "brusque" environment of Germany and instead, he decided to head to Switzerland.

"I liked the idea of the continent, but it

had to be somewhere I was comfortable with. I didn't just want to go anywhere. I decided on Switzerland, but initially I wanted to go to Basel. I went over there to talk to them, but Lucerne came in and I really liked it.

"The move was great and I loved it there, but in some ways it was a little bit too peaceful. Lucerne had beautiful forests, lakes, architecture, but just didn't have the buzz of Liverpool."

Upon leaving Lucerne, Fairclough returned to Merseyside, but within 12 months, he was off on another European jaunt.

"An offer came in from a team in Larnaca in Cyprus. The owner of the team couldn't do enough for me, but I had my doubts because it was too hot.

"Then we were on the beach one day and a big Scouse family were sitting there. They owned the famous Blue Star chippys around Liverpool and they were all going, 'come on David, you're well too good for Cypriot football,' so I decided there and then to go to Beveren."

His time in the satellite town just outside of Antwerp initially proved successful, with Beveren reaching the third round of the UEFA Cup after knocking out Athletic Bilbao.

The squad included the brother of the legendary Jean-Marie Pfaff (the former Bayern Munich keeper soon became a good friend of Fairclough's), as well as Eugene Ekeke who scored against England in the 1990 World Cup.

Fairclough's performances didn't go unnoticed and Ajax lodged a bid for the striker who was nearing his 30th birthday.

'Everywhere you go there's always a Scouser. They hunted me down wherever I went, especially in Canada'

Beveren's president rejected the offer and eventually the Dutch giants signed Frank Stapleton instead.

Within a year, Beveren's fortunes had slumped, their manager had been replaced and Fairclough was left looking for another club.

A move to French club Quimper fell through and despite interest from Bastia and Gueugnon, he eventually returned to live in Liverpool.

"The one thing I found about living abroad was that nobody understood my accent, so I had to soften it to help others. The phraseology had to change too. I'd be saying things like 'great' and 'I'm made up.' People would be like, 'What does that mean?' Even in press interviews in North America, they couldn't understand me. So I had to tone the Scouseness down a bit, so it changed my outlook on life."

Lucerne, Switzerland

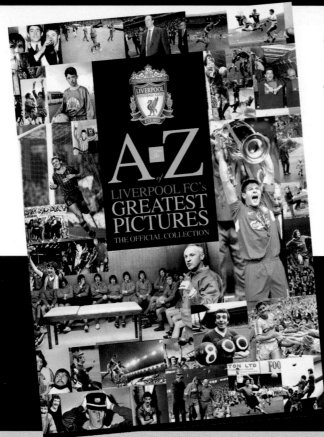

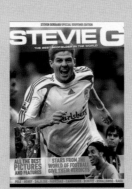

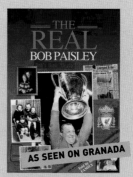

|| CAPTAIN ||

SCOUSE SKIPPERS

THERE are no captains like Scouse captains.

It is doubtful that any other city in the world had produced so many leaders with the qualities that Scousers possess.

As far back as Tom Bromilow, to Tommy Smith, then Phil Thompson and Stevie G today, each one has captured their own moment in history.

Whether it's Tommo parading the European Cup around the Parc des Princes in Paris, or Stevie punching the same trophy high into the Istanbul sky, everyone has their own memory of a Scouse captain making history.

One quality that enables Scousers to reach such halcyon nights is their tough mental and physical ability.

And they didn't come any tougher than Tommy Smith.

Smithy demanded commitment and success, and his attitude towards players who didn't is well documented.

So what made him such a good captain?

Bob Paisley on Smithy: "Tommy hated losing and was quite prepared to put himself through all manner of pain and suffering to avoid it. There was an element of notoriety about it which I think he quite enjoyed, but if any opponent cared to put

that reputation to the test, Tommy didn't disappoint them. His fearless nature not only unsettled the opposition, it inspired his team-mates. They drew strength from his example. It was a little bit like having a big brother around to sort out any trouble you got into. Seeing Tommy racing on to the field after having a couple of stitches inserted into a head wound could put courage into the most cowardly of hearts – as long as you were on his side!"

Chris Lawler on Smithy: "Tommy started out as a centre forward and I was amused by his playing style. The opposition would kick off and Smithy would be straight in to tackle the centre-half. Shouldn't it have been the other way round?"

Smithy on himself: "I was only 15 and playing in a five-a-side game at Melwood. I nutmegged Byrne and scored and I was on top of the world. A couple of minutes later a ball dropped between us, I went to head it and Gerry headed me and I went down with a gashed eye. As I lay on the ground covered in blood, Shankly strolled across, looked down at me and said `lesson number one, never nutmeg Gerry Byrne son and think you can get away with it.'"

Steven Gerrard showed his leadership on THAT night in Istanbul

'Tommy hated losing and he was quite prepared to put himself through all manner of pain and suffering to avoid it'

The Survivor of Ladispoli

by SIMON HUGHES

IN an era when celebrities use football association as a tool of convenience, it's rare to speak to someone who has been in the public eye that actually knows what they are talking about. But after several decades of following the Reds you would expect that from The Farm lead singer and über-fan Peter Hooton

HILE the Liverpool squad rested in a plush Roman hotel as they prepared for the 1984 European Cup final, thousands of Kopites descended on the surrounding Lazio region.

Those with the lire stayed in Ostia, a playground for the rich and famous. Others were lucky enough to holiday further south on the idyllic island of Capri.

Peter Hooton had the unfortunate pleasure of spending a week in Ladispoli, an Etruscan seaside commune that in Hooton's own words, "makes New Brighton look like **Las Vegas**."

"Sixty of us from the Leather Bottle pub in Halewood flew over there on the Friday before the game. It was like a 'who's who'

of Liverpool away fans. There were the so-called 'Halewood Chains,' the 'Huyton Baddies' and a smattering of people from Kirkby, Kirkdale and Bootle.

"When we arrived, we actually thought we were going to stay in Ostia, but the bus driver was adamant that it was to be Ladispoli.

"Obviously news of our arrival spread around town because within half an hour, the scooter boys had arrived and they started marking their territory by doing wheelies and leaving tyre marks.

"Soon there were about 300 locals outside Bar Internationale, the pub we were drinking in. They were just staring at us, but about 50 of these had the 'let's kill

>

the English' look about them."

Just when Hooton thought the villagers were going to act out a scene from Royston Vasey, someone appeared brandishing a gun.

"Initially we thought, 's***, they've got guns. Luckily, it was Angelo the friendly plain clothed policeman, who everyone in the town seemed to love.

"Angelo spoke English and liked us. As a gesture of reconciliation, he arranged a football match between the scooter boys and us later on in the week and a peace was found.

"The match was talk of the town and the European Cup final paled into insignificance.

"Hundreds of people turned up to watch and unsurprisingly we lost to the Italians, who were technically better than us."

This trip to the rear end of Italian holiday resorts is just one example of Hooton's commitment to following the Reds.

Since his first game in 1965, The Farm front man has done just about everything a fan can possibly do to support his team.

From hopping across the Channel for midweek European

> 'The 1980s was obviously a very depressed time for the city. Football for both clubs allowed Scousers to escape from reality. It was a safety valve'

nights to staging a one-man boycott of matches during Graeme Souness' managerial reign, Hooton has seen it all.

It was this fanaticism that drove him to create his own fanzine in the early 1980s called The End – the first publication of its kind that was written by, and for, Merseyside football supporters who followed their team home and away.

"The 80s was obviously a very depressed period for the city. Football for both clubs allowed Scousers to escape from reality. It was a safety valve. Bill Shankly always said that without football, there would be a revolution. He was right.

"During the 80s, it felt like it was Liverpool vs Thatcher every Saturday afternoon. Liverpool was the most successful team in the country. There were numerous articles in the papers that went along the line of, 'Liverpool is a deprived city…but it still has its football.'

"I didn't feel that there was a magazine that reflected young people's opinions, especially in Liverpool. There was nothing around that included things that I wanted to read or say.

They were just staring at us with that 'lets kill the English' look

Hooton joins the other writers of a book called Here We Go Gathering Cups in May about Reds fans' experiences at European Cup finals

HERE WE GO GATHERING CUPS IN MAY

"I wanted The End to appeal to both Liverpool and Everton fans who went to away matches and I think it worked. We sold it at both grounds on match days and went into the Red Brick (now the Brick), the Royal Oak and the Blue House pubs. Over the years, not one fan came up to us and said that they thought we were Reds, even though we all were. We were never partisan – not once did a Blue figure out that it was written by Reds and I was proud of that. It was about stories rather than Everton or Liverpool."

The End gave Hooton a mouthpiece to speak his mind about various issues and at its peak it sold more than 5,000 copies – no mean feat given that it was only distributed on an ad hoc basis.

The late John Peel regularly championed the fanzine live on air, describing it as 'the stuff of life. Music, football and beer.'

Although it's been 20 years since The End was last released, Hooton is still a keen reader of rival fanzines, even if they are published by Evertonians or Mancs.

"There are three fanzines around now that I like. Red All Over The Land (Liverpool), When Skies are Grey (Everton) – which is really well written – and United we Stand (Manchester Utd). If I ever see that in WHSmith, I will have a read of it, but I will never buy it for obvious reasons. I know Liverpool lads who do buy it.

"Nobody would ever buy Red Issue (Manchester Utd), unless you were short of toilet roll, but United we Stand is well written and at least they do try to write with a bit of humour instead of vitriol all the time.

"Red Issue has a very parochial view on things because most of the people who write it have probably never even met a Scouser. When we go to Old Trafford we go looking for the people who write Red Issue to give them a bit of verbal, but we never catch them. If we did, they would probably run off anyway."

Despite Hooton's obvious dislike for United, there is equally no escaping exactly how he feels about Everton.

"I know a lot of Liverpudlians who refuse to go to Goodison because they say that it's a dump and it's horrible. They say that it's like going to Galatasaray because people pretend to slit your throat. Personally, I find that funny. I don't find that threatening.

"I see the Park End tearing their hair out and a fella in his 60s who looks like the Pope marching up and down punching his hands like Mussolini. It's all frantic but for me, that's like when we used to go to Leeds and laugh at Leeds fans. When you go to Goodison now, it's because they're so demented and so obsessed with Liverpool Football Club, it's almost like a mental illness.

"It was exactly the same when we went to United in the 80s and it really reminds me of then because they were so obsessed with overtaking us with the vitriol and the bile that went with it."

Having been to nearly every Merseyside derby in the last 20 years, Hooton is perfectly placed to pass such observations.

"The rivalry has gone from the 80s when it was banter and pub violence to just pure unadulterated hatred. There's a sickening element to the rivalry now.

"It's a siege mentality. I remember when Everton fans were given the whole of the Anfield Road and we were given the Park End for away derby matches. Now fans get little sections and it adds to the animosity in a way because back then, you didn't feel like an away fan. You felt like you were

>

'The End' fanzine

in your own city and it was two big teams playing each other. If both clubs agreed to revert to that, I think it would help things, although I don't know how they'd do it because of season tickets."

There is a crude irony that the year Hooton shot to fame with Groovy Train and All Together Now was also the last year Liverpool won the title.

That makes 1990 seem a long, long time ago and he is in no doubt what led the club on a path to 17 years without league glory.

"When I grew up, I was used to success, but one man changed all that. Graeme Souness. That was it, the beginning of the end. As soon as he got the job, I wasn't happy. He'd done well with Rangers, but at the time I think I could win the league with

"When he came to Anfield, it's well documented that he tried to change a lot of things. The boot room got demolished and that was the end of it. When he sold his story to the Sun (Souness gave an exclusive to the Sun after undergoing a heart by-pass operation), I remember some Liverpudlians even half trying to defend him. There weren't many, but there were some. I started boycotting the match until he went. Looking back at it now, he's probably not that bad a person, but I just got the impression he did it for his own personal, selfish reasons.

"For me though, he should have been sacked as soon as he sold his story to the Sun. At the time, it was barely three years since Hillsborough. It was unthinkable; the longest suicide note in history.

"I couldn't bring myself to go to the matches and I stuck it out from the time he sold his story to the time he went. I'd still go the ground before a game, but I'd not go in. I just wanted to still have that feeling of being involved. It's a shame because he was a fantastic player, an absolutely brilliant player, but I couldn't watch them while he was still there. He'd still be in my all-time Liverpool XI, but he wasn't the right man for Liverpool."

> ## 'I remember when Everton fans were given the whole of the Anfield Road and we were given the Park End for derby matches. Now away fans get little sections and it adds to the animosity'

Rangers. I didn't like the type of personality he was going to bring. As soon as he signed a Catholic for Rangers, that was nothing to do with equal opportunities, that was to do with him saying 'I am Graeme Souness, I can do anything I like.' I definitely didn't read that as 'Souness the great champion of anti-sectarianism'. That was what spelt danger for me.

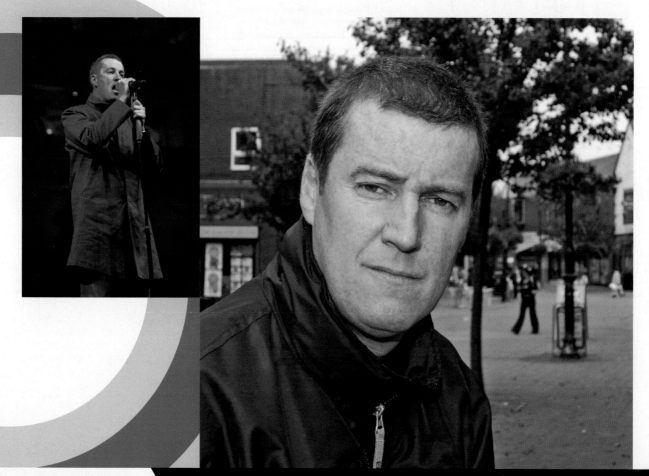

The lack of league title trophies being placed in the Anfield trophy cabinet is not the only thing to have changed about the club in recent years.

When Hooton was growing up, the Reds included a core of Scouse players in the first team squad. But since the introduction of a succession of foreign managers, Scouse heart has been replaced by a strong French, then Spanish, influence.

Hooton is philosophical on this issue.

"It is important that you have got local lads who understand the importance and heritage of Liverpool Football Club. This isn't an ordinary football club, because this is the club that Bill Shankly built. He built a dynasty and the idea was that it was going to be more than football.

"The fact that he always had local lads involved meant that they understood that, whereas if you have mercenaries who come because of money, they might be great players, but they won't understand the importance of a game against Everton or Man United and will soon get found out by the fans. I think players like Torres do. Mascherano is a Scouser at heart isn't he? Even though he's from Argentina, he could have been born in Scotland Road. He's absolutely top class.

"I was arguing recently with an Evertonian who said that Mascherano isn't as good as Hargreaves. I was thinking, do you watch football? Hargreaves for me is a decent footballer, but he's not in the same class as Mascherano. We've gotta buy him soon, otherwise I've got another boycott coming on! He wants to play for Liverpool. Even if we have to sell, we need to sign him. Argentinians and Scousers are the same breed. They say Buenos Aires, Liverpool, Marseille and Naples are all very similar cities because they are all port cities and the people are the same."

The early days of The Farm, who recorded a version of All Together Now for Everton's 1995 FA Cup song...without Peter Hooton

Why I didn't sing for Everton

ORIGINALLY released in 1990, All Together Now was re-released in 1995 as Everton's FA Cup final song. The Farm's lead vocalist explains why:

"IT'S A DIFFICULT one for me this. We'd done several things for Liverpool. We'd done the Ian Rush testimonial and a couple of other things like season review soundtracks. Then when Everton got to the cup final, we got this call from a record executive fella from London who said that he wanted to use All Together Now. I asked him what for, then he said it was for Everton's FA Cup song. My initial reaction was 'no chance'. Not because it was Everton, but mainly because it belittled the song and made it a frivolous cup final song. They're supposed to be fun songs and almost semi-joke songs. Two people in the group had sons who were 10 or 11 years old and were begging us to let them use the song because they were Blues. I got a lot of pressure from various members of the band, but I think I would have been able to withstand that.

"Then I spoke to my dad about it who has been a Liverpool season ticket holder since the 60s and he said that if I don't give it to them, it's hypocritical because of the lyrics. The lyrics are about war and passion and getting together because football unites. After two weeks of agony, I reluctantly gave in, although they had already recorded the song without me. People always say to me, 'you sang that song,' but really, I didn't. I never even went to the recording studio, I just allowed them to use it. Keith Mullin, the Evertonian, went into the studio, but he's not even a real Evertonian anyway. The lyrics were written by Joe Ainsworth, who wrote Brookside, and I just sat back and let them get on with it and it was done and dusted. If you listen, you will realise that it's Keith, who's the guitar player, actually singing the song. If I had the choice again, I would probably reject it.

"People still remind me of it, thinking it is my Achilles heel, but I just laugh about it. As soon as it was released, Billy Butler was playing it all the time and I was like 'ahh no, stop playing it.' I went into the Albert after one of the games and about 200 hardcore Liverpool fans started singing All Together Now, so I didn't know what to do. I thought that if I walked out, I'd never be able to let it go and it would be embarrassing. So I walked to the front of the bar and just made an announcement. I just said: 'Ok, I know what you're getting at. The drinks are on me.' Not one person came and took the offer up. A lot of people came up and said things like: 'Is right lad.' Knowledgable Liverpool fans don't bring it up because they all know the story now.

"People don't call me an England fan cos England have used it. There's been about 20 different techno versions, Germany used it as their anthem for the last World Cup, the homeless World Cup are using it next year and the capital of culture are using it as well, so the idea is that it's everybody's song."

The People's Republic of Merseyside

GK	Tony Warner
RB	Tony Hibbert
CB	Alan Stubbs
CB	Jamie Carragher
LB	Leighton Baines
RM	Steven Gerrard
CM	Kevin Nolan
LM	Joey Barton
F	David Nugent
CF	Robbie Fowler
F	Wayne Rooney

Subs: Ian Dunbavin (Accrington Stanley) Ryan Taylor (Wigan) Michael Ball (Man City) Lee Trundle (Bristol City) Jay McEveley (Derby County)

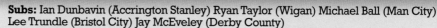

Paul Jewell (Manager)

ALL SCOUSE XI

MOST Scousers bear a sense of apathy towards the English national team.

A southern bias led by a London-based press is the general explanation for such a lack of interest.

This often makes Scousers want to follow other nations – especially during major tournaments.

At best Scousers are generally impassive towards the national team and such feelings are understandable.

Wherever England play, the absence of the unmistakable Scouse voice in the crowd is audible. As a result many Merseyside-based players have taken undue stick while wearing the three lions from fans who know little or nothing about our national sport.

But what would happen if Merseyside broke away from the crown and created its own independent breakaway state?

A People's Republic of Merseyside would replace stoicism with passion, and local pride alone would surely push us towards qualification for World Cups and European Championships.

So how do you think the side above would fare on the international stage?

Scousers
THE PEOPLE. THE PRIDE. THE PASSION.

ROYAL DAFFODIL

OUT NOW £20
(including free p&p – UK only)

WANT MORE SCOUSE PASSION?

Celebrate the amazing city of Liverpool, the architecture, the traditions, the history and the heroes...

- Over 200 pages of the famous city of Liverpool
- Taking a look at the people that make Liverpool the city it is today, from artists to musicians, innovators to public servants, including some honorary Scousers
- Great pictures taken by award winning photographers

A CITY OF AMAZING CONTRASTS

Visit **www.merseyshop.com** or call **0845 143 0001** Monday to Friday (9am-5pm) to order your copy today. Also available in all good bookshops

The full list of statistics on all Liverpool FC's Scousers

NAME	POSITION	BIRTHPLACE	D.O.B	SIGNED FROM	APPS	GLS	MOVED TO
ALAN A'COURT	LEFT-WING	RAINHILL	30.9.1934	PRESCOT CELTIC	381	63	TRANMERE ROVERS
GARY ABLETT	DEFENCE	LIVERPOOL	19.11.1965	JUNIORS	147	1	EVERTON
JOHN ALDRIDGE	STRIKER	LIVERPOOL	18.9.1958	OXFORD UNITED	104	63	REAL SOCIEDAD
JACK BALMER	STRIKER	LIVERPOOL	6.2.1916	COLLEGIATE	312	110	RETIRED
JOHN BAMBER	HALF-BACK	ST HELENS	11.4.1895	ST HELENS TOWN	80	2	LEICESTER CITY
ALAN BANKS	INSIDE-FORWARD	LIVERPOOL	5.10.1938	RANKIN BOYS	8	6	EXETER CITY
TOM BENNETT	CENTRE-MIDFIELD	LIVERPOOL	APRIL 1891	ROCHDALE	1	0	RETIRED
ARTHUR BERRY	STRIKER/WINGER	LIVERPOOL	3.1.1888	OXFORD UNI	4	0	WREXHAM
LOUIS BIMPSON	INSIDE RIGHT/CEN FWD	RAINFORD	14.5.1929	BURSCOUGH	102	39	BLACKBURN ROVERS
ROBERT BLANTHORNE	STRIKER	BIRKENHEAD	8.1.1884	BIRKENHEAD FC	2	1	GRIMSBY TOWN
PHIL BOERSMA	MIDFIELD/STRIKER	KIRKBY	24.9.1949	JUNIORS	121	30	MIDDLESBROUGH
THOMAS BRADSHAW	STRIKER	LIVERPOOL	24.8.1873	NORTHWICH VICTORIA	138	53	TOTTENHAM
TOM BROMILOW	LEFT-HALF	LIVERPOOL	7.10.1894	FREE AGENT	375	11	RETIRED
DEREK BROWNBILL	STRIKER	LIVERPOOL	4.2.1954	JUNIORS	1	0	PORT VALE
GERRY BYRNE	LEFT-BACK	LIVERPOOL	29.8.1938	JUNIORS	333	4	RETIRED
IAN CALLAGHAN	MIDFIELD	LIVERPOOL	10.4.1942	JUNIORS	857	68	FT. LAUDERDALE
BOBBY CAMPBELL	WING-HALF	LIVERPOOL	23.4.1937	JUNIORS	25	2	PORTSMOUTH
DON CAMPBELL	CENTRE-BACK/MID	LIVERPOOL	19.10.1932	JUNIORS	48	2	CREWE ALEXANDRA
JOHN CARLIN	STRIKER	LIVERPOOL	1880	LOCAL	35	8	PRESTON NORTH END
WILLIE CARLIN	INSIDE-FORWARD	LIVERPOOL	6.10.1940	LOCAL	1	0	HALIFAX TOWN
LEN CARNEY	STRIKER	LIVERPOOL	30.5.1915	COLLEGIATE	6	1	RETIRED
JAMIE CARRAGHER	DEFENCE	BOOTLE	28.1.1978	JUNIORS	502	4	N/A
JIMMY CASE	CENTRE-MIDFIELD	LIVERPOOL	18.5.1954	JUNIORS	269	46	BRIGHTON
PHIL CHARNOCK	CENTRE-MIDFIELD	SOUTHPORT	14.2.1975	JUNIORS	2	0	CREWE ALEXANDRA
FRANCIS CHECKLAND	CENTRE-BACK	LIVERPOOL	31.7.1895	JUNIORS	5	0	TRANMERE ROVERS
ALBERT CHILDS	RIGHT-BACK	LIVERPOOL	25.9.1930	NORTHERN NOMADS	2	0	RETIRED
JOHN DAVIES	STRIKER	LIVERPOOL	JULY 1881	LOCAL	10	0	BLACKPOOL
JOE DICKSON	INSIDE-RIGHT/LEFT	LIVERPOOL	31.1.1934	LOCAL	6	4	RETIRED
CYRIL DONE	STRIKER	LIVERPOOL	21.10.1920	BOOTLE BOYS BRIGADE	110	38	TRANMERE ROVERS
JOHN DURNIN	STRIKER	LIVERPOOL	18.8.1965	WATERLOO DOCK	3	0	OXFORD UNITED
ROY EVANS	DEFENCE	LIVERPOOL	4.10.1948	JUNIORS	11	0	RETIRED
DAVID FAIRCLOUGH	STRIKER	LIVERPOOL	5.1.1957	JUNIORS	154	55	TORONTO BLIZZARD
PHIL FERNS	DEFENCE	LIVERPOOL	14.11.1937	MANCHESTER CITY	28	1	BOURNEMOUTH
FRED FINNEY	DEFENCE	PRESCOT	10.3.1924	LOCAL	2	0	RETIRED
MATTHEW FITZSIMMONS	CENTRE-BACK	LIVERPOOL	10.12.1913	MATHER UNITED	1	0	IPSWICH TOWN
ROBBIE FOWLER	STRIKER	LIVERPOOL	9.4.1975	JUNIORS	369	183	CARDIFF
TOM GARDNER	HALF-BACK	HUYTON	28.5.1910	ORRELL FC	5	0	GRIMSBY TOWN
HOWARD GAYLE	STRIKER	LIVERPOOL	18.5.1958	JUNIORS	5	1	BIRMINGHAM CITY
STEVEN GERRARD	CENTRE-MIDFIELD	HUYTON	30.5.1980	JUNIORS	417	90	N/A
TOM GREEN	STRIKER	ROCK FERRY	25.11.1883	SALTNEY	7	1	SWINDON TOWN
ALF HANSON	WIDE MIDFIELD	LIVERPOOL	27.2.1912	BOOTLE	177	52	CHELSEA
CHRIS HARRINGTON	MIDFIELD	LIVERPOOL	25.12.1896	SOUTH LIVERPOOL	4	0	WIGAN BOROUGH
JOHN HEYDON	CENTRE-HALF	BIRKENHEAD	19.10.1928	EVERTON	67	0	MILLWALL
DAVE HICKSON*	STRIKER	E'SMERE PORT	30.10.1929	EVERTON	67	38	BURY
ALAN HIGNETT	FULL-BACK	LIVERPOOL	1.11.1946	LOCAL	1	0	CHESTER CITY
ALAN HIGNETT	DEFENCE	LIVERPOOL	UNKNOWN	LOCAL	1	0	RETIRED
RALPH HOLDEN	DEFENCE	B'NDELLSANDS	UNKNOWN	ST HELENS REC	2	0	TRANMERE ROVERS
JASON HUGHES	HALF-BACK	LIVERPOOL	DEC 1885	LOCAL	15	0	CRYSTAL PALACE
LAURIE HUGHES	CENTRE-BACK	LIVERPOOL	2.3.1924	TRANMERE ROVERS	326	1	RETIRED
COLIN IRWIN	DEFENCE	LIVERPOOL	9.2.1957	JUNIORS	44	3	SWANSEA CITY
NORMAN JAMES	CENTRE-BACK	LIVERPOOL	25.3.1908	BRABY'S ATHLETIC	8	0	BRADFORD CITY
DAVID JOHNSON	STRIKER	LIVERPOOL	23.10.1951	IPSWICH TOWN	213	78	EVERTON
BARRY JONES	CENTRE-BACK	PRESCOT	20.6.1970	JUNIORS	1	0	WREXHAM
HAROLD JONES	STRIKER	LIVERPOOL	22.5.1933	LOCAL	1	0	RHYL
CHARLIE JOWITT	GOALKEEPER	LIVERPOOL	1872	UNKNOWN	1	0	UNKNOWN
GEORGE KAYE	WING HALF	LIVERPOOL	19.4.1919	LOCAL	2	0	SWINDON TOWN
BRIAN KETTLE	LEFT-BACK	PRESCOT	22.4.1956	JUNIORS	4	0	WIGAN ATHLETIC
KEVIN KEWLEY	STRIKER	LIVERPOOL	2.3.1955	LOCAL	1	0	DALLAS TORNADO
FRANK LANE	GOALKEEPER	WALLASEY	20.7.1948	TRANMERE ROVERS	2	0	NOTTS COUNTY
CHRIS LAWLER	RIGHT-BACK	LIVERPOOL	20.10.1943	JUNIORS	549	61	PORTSMOUTH
SAMMY LEE	MIDFIELD	LIVERPOOL	7.2.1959	JUNIORS	295	19	QPR